D1016976

CONSULTANTS

HENRY O. GOLIGHTLY

Consultants

SELECTING, USING AND EVALUATING BUSINESS CONSULTANTS

Franklin Watts
New York/Toronto
1985

Library of Congress Cataloging in Publication Data

Golightly, Henry O.
Consultants : selecting, using, and evaluating
business consultants.

Includes index.
1. Business consultants.   I. Title.
HI69.C6G64   1985   658.4'6   85-13803
ISBN 0-531-09591-6

CONTENTS

ACKNOWLEDGMENTS

In the development of this book, I received valuable assistance from the following clients, some of whom replied to a questionnaire I sent out and with others of whom I discussed the situation: E. Garrett Bewkes, Chairman, President & CEO, American Bakeries Company; Reginald Brack, Jr., Group Vice President, Time, Inc.; Thomas T. Brekka, former Chief Financial Officer, GATX Corp.; Alexander Brody, President and CEO, DYR-Worldwide; Robert L. Crandall, Chairman & President, American Airlines, Inc.; Edgar M. Cullman, Chairman & CEO, Culbro Corporation; Alexander Damm, former President, Continental Airlines, Inc.; Samuel L. Higginbottom, Chairman & President, Rolls-Royce Inc.; Lawrence H. Lee, Chairman of the Board, Western Airlines; David J. Mahoney, former Chairman & CEO, Norton Simon, Inc.; Edward N. Ney, Chairman & CEO, Young &

Rubicam Inc.; Martin R. Shugrue, Vice Chairman, Pan American World Airways, Inc.; Robert F. Six, Chairman of the Board Emeritus, Continental Airlines, Inc.; William H. Waltrip, President & CEO, Purolator, Inc.; Thomas M. Wendel, Executive Vice President & Managing Director, Capital Markets, Financial Institutions & Market Division, Paine Webber, Inc.

The following friends made most helpful suggestions: John Gerrity, former McKinsey & Co. Partner, now Professor of Management, Yale University; Alan Ofner, former Divisional Vice President and Director of Corporate Personnel Planning, J. C. Penney Company and former fellow member of McKinsey & Co., now Consultant, Managing Change, Inc.; James M. Wainger, Principal, Harbridge House, Inc.

In particular, I want to thank Hope Raymond, who provided valuable assistance in the preparation of this book.

CONSULTANTS

This book is dedicated to
the former loyal staff of
Golightly International
(later Golightly-Harbridge)
and particularly to Elisa Cella,
who was in charge of administration
and finance, and kept the
machinery running smoothly.

It is also dedicated to
Charles D. Baker, former Chairman
of Harbridge House and
currently Under Secretary of
the U.S. Department
of Health and Human Services,
and George Rabstejnek, now
Chairman and President of
Harbridge House, who gave us
strong support after we were
acquired by Harbridge.

FOREWORD

By David J. Mahoney

Using a management consultant is like learning to ride a bicycle: if you are going to get the best results, you had better learn to do it properly.

There are good consultants, there are bad consultants, and there are lots of others in between. There are also good and bad consulting relationships. If the results a company gets from its management consultant are outstanding, it is usually because the company selected the consultant well and also because of an informed, positive working relationship between the two. Likewise, if the results are not what was anticipated, the blame should usually be shared by both the company and the consultant.

I have read this book in manuscript and find that it contains a wealth of solid advice on getting your money's worth from consultants. As C.E.O. of Norton Simon Inc. and earlier as Executive

V.P. of Colgate-Palmolive, I have used management consultants for many years. Yet, I have learned some new things in reading this book by Henry Golightly. Thus, I can say that the book will be of value to experienced users of consultants as well as to new users. It will also be informative to those in the consulting profession and to those entering or planning to enter the field.

This book contains Henry Golightly's accumulated experiences of over thirty years in the consulting field, most of which as head of a firm bearing his name. His reputation in consulting and in business in general is of the highest order.

Henry Golightly's book accurately reflects his basic integrity, critical insight and candor. He invites trust and nurtures it consistently as his book firmly but sensitively guides you through the treacherous schools of management and relationships. For over thirty years I have worked with, admired and respected the author.

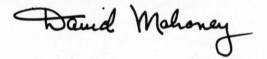

INTRODUCTION

It is estimated by ACME (the Association of Consulting Management Firms) that fees paid annually to consultants in the United States are now in the range of $6 billion—$2½ billion in the public sector and $3½ billion in the private sector. Even the late Senator Dirksen would have agreed that this is real money. Are all their clients getting full value, and if not, why not?

The evidence suggests that most of them think so. The use of consultants is increasing steadily. Management consulting as we know it today got its start in the 1930s and in only fifty years has reached its present volume, attesting to client satisfaction. As companies grow bigger and bigger and as the role of government—federal, state and local—becomes greater and greater, an even larger usage of consultants is predicted for the future.

The best guess in the industry is that 85 percent of the *Fortune* 500 companies have used or are using consultants, not just once but over and over again, to say nothing of the numerous smaller companies that require help from time to time and the governmental agencies and nonprofit organizations that depend heavily on consultants for expertise and extra manpower. The use of consultants is also growing in the United Kingdom and Germany and to a lesser extent in other Western European countries. In Japan, both Western and Japanese consulting firms are expanding at a rapid pace. Everywhere, company executives are proud of their consulting relationships and discuss them quite openly, in contrast to the secrecy that was common when I began my consulting career some thirty years ago.

Yet, there can be no doubt that some consulting assignments produce a better result than others. Every consultant and every executive knows of cases where the consultant has been able to give his client substantial help, and of others where the results of his work were something less than striking. Why is this so? Why do some consulting assignments wind up with both the consultant and the client pleased with the results, and others with concealed—or expressed—dissatisfaction on both sides?

This question is one to which I have given considerable thought. Unlike many of the present generation of consultants who go directly from graduate business schools to large consulting firms, I came into consulting as a professional in labor relations. I began my career in Texas with a construction company. My academic training was as a lawyer; my early years in industry were spent as a personnel and labor relations executive. I joined the well-known consulting firm of McKinsey & Co. in 1949 with the hope of becoming a capable general consultant. While I was a novice and needed both training and experience in consulting, I had professional skills in my own field.

It seemed to me then, and still does, that there is considerably more to consulting than arriving at an intellectual understanding of a company's problem, important though such an understanding may be. The true test of successful consulting is the action taken by the client which produces positive results.

During the years I spent with McKinsey and later as head of my own firm, Golightly & Co. International, which merged with Harbridge House in 1978, I took part in or directed hundreds of studies for clients in industries which included airlines, advertising agencies, drug companies, consumer conglomerates, large oil companies, and various other types of business. These studies varied widely in scope and subject matter, but I think that our clients would agree that most of them were successful. In a few cases, the results were unsatisfactory. In these cases, the trouble did not occur because the consultant lacked expertise or zeal. We always tried to accept only assignments for which we were qualified and to do our best for all of our clients. More often, the difficulty was traceable to the client-consultant relationship.

I have come to believe that the way in which the client analyzes his problem and then selects and works with the consultant is the single most important factor in determining the success or failure of the study. Consultants, like household robots, are not yet developed to the point where you can simply order one, turn it loose, and forget it. For good results, intelligent handling and interaction is required.

This book is intended to be a user's manual for the executive. I hope that it is comprehensive enough to be helpful to the potential first-time client, original enough to be of interest to the person who already has a sizable collection of "black books." I believe it will also prove useful to other consultants, those who plan to enter the profession, and to the many other people who come in contact with consultants in the course of their working lives.

CHAPTER

1

WHY USE
A
CONSULTANT?

During the thirty years that I have been a practicing management consultant, the reputation of consultants has improved steadily. They are now a recognized part of the business and professional community, making a solid and substantial contribution to industry, service institutions, and all levels of government.

In spite of all this, however, there is some difference of opinion about the value of consultants. In any group of executives it is usually possible to find at least one who would advise against employing them. Although we in the consulting profession naturally do not agree, we must acknowledge that occasionally the objections to consultants are well-founded.

Of course, some of the adverse criticism is merely disguised self-justification. The former company president who lost his job in a consultant-recommended reorganization will probably not feel very friendly toward the consultant who proposed the plan. This will be true even, or perhaps especially, if the president is well aware that he was spending more time on the golf course or on outside boards of directors than in running the company. Such instances are not uncommon.

Sometimes, too, the consultant is blamed on the shoot-the-messenger principle. Top management, seeing that the company is going downhill and unable to halt the slide, calls in a consultant. Shortly thereafter it is announced that a plant will be shut down, a division will be sold, and middle management will be asked to take a cut in salary. Those employees who were unaware of how badly the company's position was deteriorating may blame the consultants for the new austerity. Consultants are expendable, and it is logical for them to take the responsibility.

Sometimes consultants are resented simply because they try to change the established way of doing things. Take the case of a corporation I will call the Zero Company. The employees of Zero were smug about their product and their marketing methods, although the company had in fact fallen behind and was no longer truly competitive in the marketplace. A consultant brought in by top management recommended making substantial changes not only in the product itself but also in the way it was presented and sold. The employees, believing that "the Zero way was the only way," were considerably disturbed. Top management was forced to institute communication and training programs to get its message across and finally even to fire a few recalcitrants in order to install the new methods.

Risks Involved in Using Consultants

It is nevertheless true that, even after due allowance has been made for prejudice and misapprehension, not all complaints about consultants are invalid. There are some genuine hazards connected with their use that any potential client should consider.

Consultants May Damage Employee Morale. The mere presence of consultants, associated as they are in many people's minds with cost-reduction or reorganization studies, may be disturbing to employees. Techniques for dealing with this problem are discussed in a later chapter.

Consultants May Make Unfair Personnel Evaluations. Sometimes consultants aggravate the difficulty by meddling injudiciously with personnel problems. The consultant is flattered when the client asks what he thinks about "old Joe." "Is he getting the job done?" It is a wise consultant who says, "I don't have enough information to evaluate his performance. I don't know all of the reasons why he may not be performing as he should, and, in fact, I don't know that he isn't." It is never a good idea for a consultant to participate in personnel evaluation, unless that is the primary purpose of the study and sufficient information is available to make a judgment. Hasty and uninformed evaluations are unfair to the employee as well as to the consultant, whose services as an unbiased observer are considerably depreciated if he or she accepts the role of management hatchet man.

Some Consultants May Have a Condescending Attitude. Sometimes consultants take a haughty attitude, particularly toward middle management. They seem to feel that their knowledge and capabilities make them superior to the middle-level employee, and sometimes even to top management. This quickly becomes known and resented. It has always been a mystery to me why some consultants appear to believe that, because a company has a problem, its employees are all unqualified and their opinions are of little value.

There may be many reasons besides management incompetence for a company's difficulties. Consultants should understand that they are brought in to help, not to create more problems. I would advise getting rid of the haughty type of consultant.

Consultants May Change Established Behavior Patterns. Even the wisest and most tactful consultant will inevitably upset established behavior patterns to some extent. For instance, consultants normally have access to upper levels of management and frequently bypass lower-level executives. Top management usually approves of the direct approach, since the purpose of engaging the consultant was to get his or her opinion, but this flouting of the chain of command may be disturbing to the executive, who cannot ignore it. Also, as previously pointed out, the consultant's recommendations may cause other cultural jarrings. The consultant may recommend changes that go against company concepts and traditions hallowed by time and habit.

Consultants May Make Ill-considered Recommendations. Consultants may be tempted to demonstrate that they have done something, even at the expense of the company's best interests. For example, a consultant who was brought in because he has a reputation for lowering costs may find many opportunities for cost-cutting, although some of the actions recommended may damage the company's future health.

Consultants Have Authority But No Real Responsibility. Consultants assume authority without responsibility. They almost always recommend change of one type or another, without having any real accountability for results. Of course, their reputations are on the line and will ultimately be damaged if their recommendations are consistently unsound, but that does not pose an immediate problem to them. It is management that will be held responsible if the plans fail.

Consultants May Take Assignments They Cannot Handle. Sometimes the consultant selected may not be qualified, and may have only superficial knowledge of the problem area. Company employees soon realize this and question management's judgment in selecting and continuing to use the consultant. Careful selection should largely eliminate this problem. Some useful selection techniques are described later in this book.

Consultants Are Expensive. A topflight consultant or consulting firm charges substantial fees. Although we in the profession like to think that our services are more than worth what they cost, there is no denying that payments to a consultant can be a noticeable item in the company budget.

Use of Consultants May Obscure the Need For Additional Company Staff. A company should have its own staff to deal with situations where there is a recurring need or where support and services would be best supplied by company personnel. It is damaging both to the consultant and to the company for the consultant to work outside the proper sphere. The person should not become a permanent fixture.

From the foregoing list of dangers, it should be obvious that the engagement of a consultant ought not to be undertaken casually. The wrong consultant not only may waste the company's time and money, but may actually do it harm.

Benefits from the Use of Consultants

While it is true that the wrong consultant may be more of a liability than an asset, the right one can help in ways that almost no one else can. No matter how capable a company's executives may be, there are many situations in which the use of a good consultant is the quickest and best method of getting the company on track.

Consultants Bring Fresh Ideas to the Company. In this era of rapid growth of corporate enterprise and vast changes in technology that can and do alter work processes, many companies need new and fresh ideas. These can include the introduction of new products, new manufacturing techniques, new marketing methods, or fundamental changes in the way the company is using its resources. Consultants can bring new concepts to the table. They are not tied to the traditional thinking that often inhibits company management.

The recent changes at Sears exemplify consultant-assisted company growth. According to a recent article in *Time*, the well-known consulting firm, McKinsey & Co., has been influential in developing new ideas for the better utilization of Sears's assets. Sears's highly profitable venture into insurance through Allstate has been extended to other financial services, real estate, and a world trading company. While the outcome of some of these ventures is still uncertain, overall they have provided highly successful uses for the company's resources. Many other companies have expanded into new areas of business with assistance from consultants.

Consultants Can Be Catalysts For Change. Even where operating management has bold new ideas, it is frequently difficult for them to put these ideas into practice. As Machiavelli said, "There is nothing more difficult to carry out, nor more doubtful of success, nor more dangerous to handle, than to initiate a new order of things." The consultant can evaluate what will be involved in implementing a change, whether it involves the consultant's own concepts or management's, assist in translating new ideas into reality, and cut through layers of management and get action at the level where it is needed. If especially wise and able, the consultant can get the employees to understand the need for change, be a part of it, and support the concepts.

When the changes involve the mergers, acquisitions, or divestitures so common today, consultants are ideally positioned to assist. They can help to identify desirable acquisitions or companies with which to merge. They can also help with the negotiations and with putting the companies together, as well as with identifying divisions or parts of the companies that are not compatible and finding other companies that are interested in acquiring them.

Consultants Are a Ready Source of Expertise. No matter what sort of difficulty management may be facing, it is almost always possible to find a highly qualified consultant who has experience in dealing with similar problems. Although management requires solutions that are applicable to its particular company, environment, and industry, and each situation is unique, the good consultant can apply general knowledge to develop a solution that will fit the needs of the client company.

The Use of Consultants Is Often Economical. Managements may find that it is actually cheaper to call in a consultant when special problems arise than to build up an internal staff large enough to deal with any contingency. The consultant's cost can be easily determined, his or her undivided attention to the problem will be obtained, and he or she can be eliminated without difficulty when the task is accomplished. In contrast, estimates of the cost of developing a solution through the use of company staff may not include overhead or other hidden items. Furthermore, the attention of company employees can easily be diverted from problem solving to other activities.

Consultants Are Solution-Oriented. Consultants can usually identify needs for change more quickly than company management. They move toward problem solving rather than toward maintaining the existing culture. They are not dedicated to the *status quo*.

All in all, there is no question that consultants can and do serve many useful purposes. I am convinced that their use will continue to increase in future years as company managements must deal with ever more complex environments.

CHAPTER

2

WHAT DOES
A
CONSULTANT
DO?

Some years ago, at the beginning of my consulting career, I went back to my home town in Texas for a visit. While there I made a trip to the local grocery with my aunt. As we were gathering supplies, we were approached by a contemporary of my aunt's who had known me as a small boy.

"And what does Henry do?" said this lady, after an exchange of greetings.

My aunt spoke quickly, before I could reply. "Henry is a lawyer," she said, jabbing me in the ribs. The lady departed, satisfied.

"Why did you say that?" I said. "You know I don't practice law."

"Henry," said my aunt, "management consulting is just too difficult to explain."

Even in more sophisticated circles, consulting is not always well understood. When I tell casual acquaintances that I am a management consultant to business, they are likely to assume that my clients are companies in trouble or facing failure. When I say that, on the contrary, almost all of the clients are successful companies that want to do even better, I often meet expressed or unexpressed skepticism.

What, in fact, does a management consultant do? One of the dictionary definitions of consultant is "One who gives professional advice or service." I would define a management consultant as one who, for a fee, gives professional advice or provides services to managements of business, government, or nonprofit organizations.

The consulting process begins when the potential client identifies a deficiency or a need for improvement in some area of the organization and decides that, for one reason or another, it is desirable to get outside help. The client thereupon discusses these needs with one or more professional consultants, eventually reaching an agreement with one of them on the nature of the work to be done, the results expected, and the amount of the consultant's fee. (Fees, which are usually based on a daily rate, are more fully discussed in the next chapter.)

The consultant will probably begin drawing up a study plan which will describe how he expects to secure the necessary data and develop his conclusions and recommendations. The consultant will probably interview executives in the department or departments affected and lower-level employees, meeting informally with the client from time to time to discuss what has been learned and the tentative conclusions that have been reached. At the end of this fact-finding period, the consultant will develop a written report embodying his or her findings on the problem and recommendations for dealing with it, and will present this report in a formal meeting, or series of meetings, with the client and other executives. If the original agreement so specifies or if a supplementary agreement has been made with the client, the consultant will assist in putting the recommendations into practice.

The consultant may work in almost any functional area with which management is concerned. Of course, no individual consultant is qualified in every field. A single consultant may perform an organizational study or a strategic planning study involving the entire company but will probably use several consultants on the project with knowledge of specific activities. It is estimated that there are now over 3,500 consulting firms in the United States, and many times that number of individual practitioners. With so many to choose from, there is seldom any great difficulty in locating a competent consultant, whatever the nature of the problem may be.

Clients may call upon consultants to assist with anything from developing an organization plan for the entire company to preparing a new marketing plan, setting up Japanese-style Quality Circles, evolving an incentive-oriented compensation plan, or providing a computer-based system for production scheduling, to mention a few of the possibilities.

If you are thinking of engaging a consultant, you will want to consider the various types of consulting firms and services available. You can then select the type that best suits your needs, taking into consideration the nature of the problem, the type of business involved, the size of the company, and the geographical area to be covered—international, national, regional, or local.

Types of Consulting Firms

Consulting firms (and individual consultants) may be loosely divided into four classes: general management consultants, functional specialists, industry specialists, and local, regional, or foreign consultants.

General Management Consultants. The distinguishing characteristics of the general management firms are that they look at problems from the overall company point of view and that they are usually capable of providing services in a number of functional areas.

James O. McKinsey, the founder of McKinsey & Co., was an early advocate of the holistic approach, which involves looking at all of the company's activities before tinkering with any of its parts. This method was originally known as the "top management approach." When the problem has not been clearly identified and it is uncertain what function or functions may be involved in its solution, such an approach has a great deal to recommend it. Only a general management firm has the resources to carry out this kind of wide-ranging study.

Some top management consulting firms that were once chiefly known as generalists, such as McKinsey and Booz Allen & Hamilton, have added so many functional and specialized services that they can now compete with the specialist firms. On the other hand, some firms that were first known as specialists have multiplied their services so that they may now be classified as general management consultants. For instance,

Arthur D. Little, Inc., once best known for its technical expertise, has extended its practice to provide a large number of managerial services as well. It may now be described as a general management firm. Another example of this process has been furnished by the Boston Consulting Group, which became known originally for its innovative approach in developing strategic plans. BCG now provides services in a variety of areas and may also be placed among the generalists.

Specialists. Specialist firms offer services or provide systems in one field, or in several related fields, designed to improve performance of a single company function or activity. There are specialists available in almost every conceivable phase of company operations. The specialists have developed in-depth skills and sophisticated systems that, with some modification, can be used by many companies. They have up-to-date information about the latest developments in their areas of specialization and know which type of plan, policy, or system offers the best solution in a given situation. When the company's problem is well defined and restricted to a single area or function, a specialist-consultant is often an excellent choice.

The work of the specialist in one management area can improve the performance of the company as a whole. For example, a data base can provide the framework for a number of systems. It can provide information for a control system that measures performance versus plan for every department or function; a materiel system that permits adequate support at optimum levels; or a personnel system that provides accurate, readily available information about the status, performance and capabilities of employees. A cost-reduction study in manufacturing that brings about an immediate reduction in costs can be a lifesaver for the entire company.

There are many specialized firms with excellent capabilities in their fields. The successful performance of these firms can be easily documented.

Some specialists are individuals: college professors, retired executives, professionals (economists, psychologists, labor lawyers, etc.), or executives out of work. Although these individual consultants may have great skills in their areas of specialization, they are not always able to apply them in a client situation so as to get results. It is this ability to get results that makes a consultant valuable.

Of course, many individual consultants do have this ability and are extremely successful. Perhaps the best known individual consultant is Peter Drucker, the guru of management methods and practices, who is a consultant to many leading companies as well as a prolific author. Drucker is extremely skillful in both diagnosis and implementation.

Industry Specialists. Certain industries have special characteristics that make their needs unique. Among these industries are retailing, banking, health care, hotels, utilities, and airlines and other modes of transportation. A company in such a field is likely to turn for help to a consultant who specializes in serving its industry.

The industry specialists are most helpful when the problem involves the factors that apply particularly to the special field. For example, in retailing, buying is a critical factor—buying that considers not only value but, very importantly, consumer trends and fashion changes.

Industry specialists are usually repositories of information about industry requirements, practices, and performance results. They should have the expertise necessary to improve company planning and performance. Since they have ba-

sic research data at hand, they can often provide
quick solutions to pressing problems.

Local, Regional, and Foreign Consulting Firms.
When a company requires information about
marketing in a specific locality, or about local
laws and methods of dealing with government
officials, it may be best served by a consultant
based in the locality in question.

These local, regional, or foreign firms are likely
to have in-depth knowledge of consumer habits,
market trends, and channels of distribution in their
areas. They should understand the legal systems
under which they operate and be able to get along
with local governments. Of course, many of the
larger consulting firms operate nationwide and
abroad and can compete with the local firms in
areas where they have set up branch offices.

One of the advantages of employing a firm that
has its office in the area where the work is to be
done is that the client will not end up paying for
extensive consultant travel and living expenses.

Kinds of Services Consultants Supply

No one person could know all the different sorts
of projects that consultants have undertaken, or

list them even if they were known. However, a great many consulting assignments do fall into certain broad areas. It may be helpful to describe some of the types of studies that consultants perform most frequently.

General Audit. A general audit is one of the most sweeping of all consulting studies. It involves an examination of each company activity to evaluate the need for it, determine whether it is being performed effectively, and recommend what can be done to improve its performance if it is to be retained.

Such audits are not usually directed to changing the main thrust of a company's activities, but rather to improving its performance in its present areas of business.

Strategic Planning Studies. The development of a strategic plan involves the overall appraisal of a company or a division to determine whether it is making optimum use of its assets and capabilities. The formulation of such a plan requires in-depth knowledge of a company's strengths, its liabilities, its products and their viability, the capabilities of its management, the abilities of its suppliers and competitors, its place in the market, and many other related matters. This knowledge is used to determine in what directions the company should go to reach its full potential and what actions will be needed to attain its goals. Such a study may lead a company to enter entirely new areas while maintaining its existing business, or it may lead to the elimination of parts of the business.

Because strategic plans can be used to project the company's future requirements, they have virtually supplanted what used to be known as long-range planning.

A good example of a successful strategic planning study is the one performed a few years ago for American Standard when William A. Marquard took over as its President. Upon taking office, Mr. Marquard found himself in charge of a whole portfolio of subsidiary companies that had been added over the years to the company's basic plumbing and heating business. Some of the subsidiaries seemed to be awkward fits, and some were losing money. He felt that consolidation of the corporation was necessary and that a number of the businesses should be disposed of.

Mr. Marquard engaged a well-known consulting firm to confirm his thinking and to develop a strategic plan. After carefully studying the problem, the consultant recommended retaining its basic businesses, disposing of the unrelated and unprofitable subsidiaries, and acquiring others more compatible with its principal activities. This strategy was adopted. The company has since enjoyed more than a decade of increased growth and profits.

The various types of consulting studies, like so many other things, tend to go in and out of fashion. At the moment, strategic planning studies are not as popular as they once were. However, the need for sound business strategy is as great as ever. In my opinion, a company's strategic plan should be brought up-to-date every few years.

Organization Planning. Organization planning can be one of the most useful tasks that consultants undertake. The development of an organization plan requires knowledge and consideration of a company's culture, its performance capabilities, and of the factors critical to its success. It involves the grouping of company activities into logical units, establishing their reporting relationships, and defining the authority and responsibility assigned to each unit. A good organization plan should also spell out the interrelationships of the various units and take into consideration the main thrust of the company, so that responsibility for the factors critical to its success is placed high in the organization structure. For example, if the company is heavily dependent on marketing, the activities that affect marketing should be given great importance and should report to top levels of the management structure.

Mature companies often find themselves working with somewhat impractical organization structures. In their early years, companies tend to develop structures based not on logic but on the strengths and weaknesses of their key executives. These structures work reasonably well as long as the original incumbents are in place, but as time goes by and other executives take over, problems are likely to arise. The company goes on following the pattern after the reason for it is forgotten.

We once had a client company, for instance, that had built its structure around a weak top financial officer and a strong general counsel. The audit function had been moved to the legal department, where it would have the benefit of the general counsel's direction. In the course of time both incumbents left their positions, but internal audits continued to be the responsibility of the legal department. At the time we were called in, the company had a strong financial officer who was unable to detect problems before they developed because the auditing function was not under his control, and he did not have a close working relationship with it.

A good consultant should be able to develop and introduce a sound, logical organization plan which, while it incorporates all the necessary changes, can be easily understood and will cause a minimum of disruption. Employee acceptance of the plan is as important as the soundness of its structure.

The consultant will also point out to management what qualifications are necessary for successful performance in each key position. Of course, the actual selection of the key executives is the responsibility of management.

Financial Studies. Most financial studies are directed toward improving the company's financial planning and control. The activities covered will probably include planning cash flow versus cash requirements, equity financing, and the negotiation of loans from banks and other lending institutions, as well as the development of policies and plans for budgeting and control of income. Tax planning, insurance, and pensions are usually also included.

Adequate financial planning and control are crucial to a company's success. It sometimes happens, however, that the importance of these functions is not appreciated until the company finds itself in difficulty. Not long ago two companies with which I am familiar came to grief through inattention to proper planning and control.

In the first case, a new chief executive of a successful company replaced a tight cost-control system under corporate supervision with a looser system that gave most of the financial responsibility to division managers. Within two years the company's financial performance had deteriorated to a point where its bank credit was withdrawn. The company had to be sold.

In the second case, the company made heavy investments with borrowed capital at a fluctuating rate of interest. When interest rates rose and a recession squeezed earnings, the bank with which it was dealing refused to extend it further credit. At that point the company called in a consultant. He recommended selling some of the company assets to raise cash for immediate needs, and also set up a tighter system of cost control.

The company survived the crisis and returned to profitability after a few years.

Human Resources Studies. A company's human resources, of course, are its employees. Consulting work in the human resources area involves the staff functions of a company relating to employees, such as manpower requirement forecasts, executive succession plans, employment, promotion, training and development, productivity improvement, communications, labor relations, compensation and benefits, and participative Quality Circle plans.

Organization planning may be included among the human resources functions, but is not always so considered.

There is no consulting firm with which I am familiar that provides services in all the human resources areas. Consultants tend to specialize in certain phases of human resources activity.

There are a number of psychologically oriented firms that develop criteria for selection and promotion of employees, perform employee attitude surveys, and evaluate employee potential.

Firms like Harbridge House specialize in management training, executive development, organization development, and other services to improve employee performance.

Compensation and benefits are a field in themselves. Consulting firms that specialize in this area are prepared to advise on equitable salary structure, bonus plans, stock option plans, pensions, and various other benefits. Insurance is usually a separate specialty.

Labor relations services, such as the negotiation of contracts, are frequently provided by legal firms that concentrate on this kind of work. Such firms usually take no part in educating field management in the interpretation of union contracts or in efforts to improve company-employee relations.

There has been a great deal of interest recently in systems to improve communications between management and employees similar to the Japanese Quality Circles system. These systems should lead to better control of quality and improved productivity. To be successful, they must not only be endorsed by top management but also be understood by management and workers at all levels, and care must be used in developing, installing, and administering them.

In selecting a consultant to assist in installing

these plans, some degree of caution is advisable. This type of system is so much in fashion that many newcomers who may or may not be fully qualified have entered the field. A well-established firm with psychological capabilities is likely to be the best candidate.

Marketing. Marketing consultants concern themselves with all the activities that affect the sale of company products, including:

The product itself — age in the marketplace, need for updating or improvement, and need for new products.

Pricing — with particular attention to competitive prices for similar products and price-to-sales ratios.

Distribution — offering the product through the proper channels; insuring that distributors are providing proper sales support and covering important markets.

Advertising and Promotion — support to secure consumer awareness and acceptance.

Customer service — important to the sale of most products, but particularly important in the service industries. Credit availability is a significant factor.

Selling — varies with the type and cost of the product line. Direct selling is important to high-value products, particularly to those that require technical knowledge, such as computers. Sales of low-cost soft goods depend largely on successfully distributing the company's products in the proper channels, plus advertising and promotion.

There are consulting firms that provide skills, know-how, and services for the entire gamut of marketing activities. Others specialize in selected functions, such as selling, market research, pricing, or product development. They all should help their clients recognize changing conditions in the marketplace and make the most of their opportunities. The right consultant can often assist a client in increasing sales and profits substantially.

Manufacturing. A manufacturing consultant may assist with improvements in any activity that has to do with making the company's products. Such work may involve the company's manufacturing plan, equipment, work standards, manufacturing methods, employee training, cost reduction, materiel planning and control, automation, the use of robots and computers, plant layout, or any other activity that impacts manufacturing effectiveness.

"Manufacturing has long been the forgotten child of industry," says Dr. Stanley Miller, a former Harvard professor who is currently a management consultant. It is not unusual for a U.S. company's equipment, plants, and manufacturing methods to be inferior to those of its international competitors. The U.S. auto industry's recent experience with the Japanese is an obvious case in point. Many U.S. companies are today in need of all the help they can get in this area to maintain their present positions or move ahead in the marketplace.

There are a number of excellent, long-established consulting firms that specialize in manufacturing and distribution problems. Lately, general management consulting firms have also been building up their capabilities in this area.

Cost-Reduction Studies. Cost-reduction studies are always popular. Even when times are good, many such studies are initiated by companies hoping to find more effective and less costly ways of doing business. During a recession, cost reduction seems even more urgent.

When a company must find a way to reduce costs, management usually takes a few obvious first steps. (We call them "home cooking.") They normally begin by reducing the number of employees, but they may also cut advertising, materiel or real estate expenses. If further reductions seem necessary, a consultant is likely to be brought in. The consultant, with knowledge of efficiency techniques and systems, will presumably be able to make recommendations for overlooked and/or innovative methods that will bring costs down with a minimum of disruption.

There are consulting firms that specialize in cost-reduction studies; some concentrate on a single function, such as manufacturing. General management firms also perform these studies. In fact, most consulting studies, regardless of their primary objective, give secondary attention to cost-reduction opportunities.

Systems. So many different types of systems are in use today, and so many different types of consultants may be involved in installing or improving them, that it is difficult to say anything sensible about the subject in a few paragraphs. The current definition of a business system is "any organized interacting activity that is used to improve performance or provide information about a company function or functions." Systems are involved when an airline makes reservations, or a manufacturing plant controls materiel supplies, or a finance department warns an advertising department that it is exceeding budget. Systems is a favorite word in today's business jargon. Every type of business activity has a system to provide information, guide performance, and/or evaluate results.

Consultants specializing in this field are able to provide systems directed to almost all management functions, including personnel, accounting, finance, work measurement, materiel management, marketing, manufacturing or operations, and many others.

These consultants can supply a system that has already been developed, work out a new system, or modify an existing one. Different consultants specialize in different kinds of systems—personnel, marketing, materiels, etc. General management consultants also have the capability to develop and install systems.

Data Processing. The computer has revolutionized the way in which data can be processed and correlated. Today almost all management systems, and many other management activities as well, involve the use of computers, but computer-based data processing as a management function is still relatively new and not always perfectly understood. Consultants expert in the data-processing field can be helpful in several areas, including:

Determining hardware needs

Establishing the organization of the data systems department and its relationship to other departments

Deciding how best to serve the requirements of the various company departments or functions needing computer-based information

Defining the role that the user departments should play in determining their requirements for data and in developing software

Selling data systems and services

Acquisitions, Mergers, and Divestitures. As
mentioned in the opening chapter, consultants
are ideally placed to assist with mergers, acquisitions, and divestitures. Many independent consultants devote themselves solely to this type of
activity and some general management firms have
divisions that specialize in it.

A consultant who is assisting with a merger or
acquisition program usually begins by conducting a study of the client company to determine
its strengths and weaknesses, such as management capabilities, physical and cash resources,
liabilities, earnings record, market position, tax
position, and future outlook. This information is
used as a guide in determining what type of company would be a suitable partner or subsidiary.

Sometimes the consultant may be used to
identify and contact desirable companies, and to
participate in or conduct the negotiations with
them. (In that case, the fee arrangements vary
from the norm: the consultant will probably be
paid a certain percentage of the purchase price
as a finder's fee.) In any case, the consultant will
probably evaluate the proposed acquisition or

merger partner in much the same way that he or she analyzed the client company. The consultant may also recommend the optimum organization for the combined companies and make suggestions on policies in other areas, such as personnel, labor relations, public relations, etc.

Consultants are usually not used to develop policies for warding off unwanted acquirers. Lawyers normally provide this type of counsel.

Candidates for divestiture are usually identified when the consultant is doing a study of the client company.

Executive Recruiting. Consultants who devote themselves chiefly to finding suitable candidates for executive vacancies differ from most other consultants in that they spend a large percentage of their consulting time in their own offices, locating prospects and conducting preliminary interviews.

Before beginning a search, however, a consultant must learn all about the position to be filled: its reporting relationships, title, duties, compensation, and opportunities for promotion and growth; and the company's requirements in terms of education, experience, and personal characteristics. In addition, the consultant must become familiar with the internal environment of the company, including its reputation as a place to work, its turnover record, and the presence or absence of internal candidates for the position who are likely to resent an outsider. Some executive search firms insist on interviewing any internal candidates before undertaking a search to determine whether it is really necessary to go outside for a candidate.

The qualified search consultant seeks to provide an exact "fit"—the executive who meets all requirements and not only *can* but *does* perform to produce the results that the company expected.

Because of the conditions under which executive recruitment is carried out, fees are based on a percentage of salary rather than on time expended. Fee structures are discussed more fully in a later chapter.

Many consulting firms devote themselves solely to executive recruiting. General management consultants often have recruiting divisions.

Consulting Is an Interactive Process

No matter what type of consultant you may engage or what kind of project that person is working on, you can never get the most out of a consultant by passive acceptance of his recommendations. You must absorb and act on the recommendations to produce results.

Working with a consultant is not always an unalloyed joy. Although you will probably welcome him or her at first, you may be tired of the consulting process by the time the study is completed. Other company executives may resent the probings. You may be told things that are not pleasing or complimentary to your own performance. Even though, as your mother used to tell you as she prepared to spank you, "it's for your own good," you may not find it easy to accept the consultant's findings.

Furthermore, the recommendations can seldom be implemented without extra effort on your part. Some company employees may not be happy with the actions you take to put the recommendations into effect, even though they are for the good of the company. You may have to secure the approval of the chief executive officer or even the board of directors. You may have to fend off detractors from other departments.

Then, too, there is always some element of risk. "What if the consultant is wrong, even though I agree with what he wants to do?" Once implemented, the recommendations might even turn out to be harmful and/or expensive.

On the other hand, inaction can be risky also. If you have the courage of your convictions and take actions you believe in, you may find that they produce many benefits.

Consider the case of Company A and Company B. Twenty years ago, these companies, in the same business with the same or similar products, and serving the same geographic area, were comparatively equal in sales and earnings. At that time, Company A, on the advice of a consultant, began to build management strength at lower levels. This involved some risk, because important authority was delegated to lower level executives who were not always fully competent. Nevertheless, Company A's supervisors and managers accepted the challenge and improved their management capabilities consistent with their newly assigned authority.

Company B did not follow this path. It continued to make most decisions at corporate level and delegated very little. It did nothing to build a strong management substructure.

Today Company A is far ahead of Company B in sales and profits, and has the internal capabilities to continue to grow and expand. Its management strength, particularly in its infrastructure, is recognized by its entire industry.

A consultant can provide the frank, unbiased, and objective opinions that most of us need to improve our own performance, and our company's. This is one of the reasons that the use of consultants continues to grow.

CHAPTER

3

ARE CONSULTANTS TOO EXPENSIVE –OR PRICELESS?

One often hears executives say, "I can't use consultants. They cost too much."

There is no denying that topflight consultants, like other professionals, sometimes charge what seem at first glance to be frighteningly high fees. An executive who hears that a consultant's fees are $1,000 to $2,000 per day may be stunned. He doesn't always stop to think what he will be getting for the money.

As everyone who has dealt with consultants knows, their normal practice in submitting a proposal to a potential client is to specify the professional fee for carrying out the assignment. This amount, plus out-of-pocket expenses, should be all that you, the client, pay unless the assignment is extended or changed. Whether you get your money's worth, or less, or more, depends on you, the consultant, and the situation.

How Fees Are Determined

The fee quoted in the proposal is usually based on the number of consulting days that the consulting firm expects the job to require, multiplied by the daily rates to be charged for the services of the consultant or consultants involved. Since the fees it charges are the firm's only source of income, the firm must be sure that they are adequate to cover its expenses and provide quality work.

The daily rate of a consultant is based on his or her salary. Our firm estimates that a consultant will be available to work on client assignments for about two hundred days a year. To arrive at the daily rate, we therefore divide the consultant's yearly salary by two hundred and then multiply the resulting figure by a factor of 2½ to 3½ to cover the costs of administration, office space, research, training, downtime (when the consultant is not working), bonuses, pensions, and benefits, and to provide for profit.

To illustrate: An employee earns $60,000 per year in salary. Divide the salary by two hundred planned work days, and we get an actual cost of $300 per planned working day. To allow for all other hidden costs and to provide for profit, we multiply $300 by 250 percent to 350 percent to get a billable daily rate of $700 to $1,050 per day. The fluctuations depend largely on the skills of the consultant concerned and his or her familiarity with the client problem.

When a firm is able to keep its consultants employed for 80 percent of their time, it makes a reasonable profit. If they work less than that, the firm makes less profit or suffers a loss. If more, a good profit is earned.

Another commonly employed method of computing the daily rate is to take the total actual cost of the consultant—that is, base salary and all fringe benefits—and divide that by the days or weeks the consultant will probably work to determine actual daily or weekly costs. Add to this a percentage of departmental costs—rent, labor, and administration. To this add another percentage for overall general administrative costs and to this add a percentage for profits. This method produces about the same billable rate as the one first described.

Using either method, the daily rate for a senior consultant will range from $700 to $1,200 in most prestigious firms in the East. There may be lower levels in locations where salaries and overhead costs are not so high. The rates of partners of leading firms will range from $1,500 to $2,500 per day or more.

Need the Rates Be So High?

Consultants' charges are substantial. It should be borne in mind, however, that a consultant may be called upon to solve the most important problems of major industries or branches of government. Therefore, senior consultants must be of top-management caliber. In their fields of expertise they should be better qualified than their industry counterparts. To retain the services of such people, consulting firms must provide salaries and benefits commensurate with those paid by industry.

Even the junior consultants employed by the more prestigious firms are highly trained and come expensive. Today, many consulting firms are in large part training their own staffs by bringing in graduates of the leading business schools and providing them with in-house experience. This puts the consulting firms in competition with industry recruiters.

In the East, the market is very competitive for the business school graduates of Harvard, Wharton, Columbia, Dartmouth, and MIT, with

Harvard graduates the most sought after. In 1983, 6.5 percent of the graduating class of the Amos Tuck School at Dartmouth went into consulting at salaries ranging from $32,000 to $50,000 a year, the mean salary being $40,080. In 1984 from Harvard, 19 percent of the MBA's went into consulting for a total of 111, with a median salary of $52,000. The range was from $24,000 to $65,000. In 1983, at the University of Virginia, the mean salary for business school graduates entering the consulting field was $40,000 a year, with a range of from $24,000 to $57,500.

Business school graduates from universities in other parts of the country, particularly Stanford, Chicago, and Northwestern, are also being actively recruited at similar salary levels.

The high rate paid to beginners means that the salary levels of senior consultants must be adjusted upward to compensate them properly and provide an appropriate salary spread of differentiation. This will mean that the experienced consultant will receive more than $60,000 annually, probably something in the $65,000 to $100,000 range. This salary will, of course, be reflected in the rate charged to clients.

The overhead costs of consulting firms are not negligible. A firm must have its offices in a convenient location in the city, where rental costs are usually high. The quarters must be similar to those of other professional firms, and include nicely furnished offices with adequate clerical and research support. The day of the consultant bull pen is largely over; each consultant is usually provided with a private office, or at least a cubicle, where one can work in private and be undisturbed. As in other professions, the higher up the ladder one goes, the larger the office and the more personalized the support services.

The firm also needs to provide research in certain management areas to keep itself up-to-date and ahead of competitors, and to provide training for its personnel. Employee benefits, including insurance, both health and life, should equal those of progressive commercial companies. On top of all this, there are the general administrative costs, including the overall management of the firm and the necessary support staff.

From all of the foregoing, it can be seen that good consulting firms do not charge high fees simply out of greed.

Executive Search Fees

The charges for an executive search are not computed in the same way as other consulting fees.

They are based on the salary, or more frequently nowadays on the total compensation, of the executive to be placed. The usual charge is 30 percent of the first year's compensation, but it varies from 25 percent to 33⅓ percent.

Most executive search firms do not work on speculation. They usually charge the client a monthly fee to cover costs of the consultant's time, to be deducted from the end fee. Some firms bill one-third of the total fees when they receive the request for the search, another one-third in thirty days, and the final one-third when one of their candidates is hired.

In addition, the client is charged on a monthly basis for out-of-pocket expenses connected with the search, such as travel, telephones, and so on.

Finder's Fees

Consultants assisting with mergers and acquisitions sometimes work for a finder's fee rather than at daily rates. This type of reimbursement is customary when the consultant identifies and contacts desirable companies and participates in or conducts the actual negotiations. The consultant is usually paid a percentage of the purchase price that gets smaller as the price increases. Something in the neighborhood of 3 percent to 5 percent for the first million, tapering down to 1 percent, would be a fairly typical fee.

Independent Consultants

The independent consultant may have a lower daily billing rate than a comparable consultant employed by a large firm. There are several reasons for this. First of all, the independent consultant may work out of the home or a small office and have few overhead costs, except telephone, utilities, and clerical or stenographic services. Also, the need for bonuses, retirement, and vacations may not be considered in determining the fee.

The potential client, of course, must give very careful consideration to the abilities of the independent consultant, since there is no one to complain to if the work is unsatisfactory. The client must also consider what would occur if the consultant were ill or otherwise unable to work after the study had begun.

In spite of the potential drawbacks, there are many independent consultants who do a top-class, professional job at relatively low rates.

Some independent consultants are recognized authorities in their own fields and charge a great deal more than consulting firms do. The prime example of this is Peter Drucker, who is well known as an economist and organization specialist. Former Secretary of State Henry Kissinger is said to be providing consulting services at high fees. There are numerous others in this category.

Billing Practices

The common practice of major consulting firms is to estimate the total costs for professional services for an assignment in advance and bill the client monthly as costs are incurred.

There are so many variables in the client situation, particularly with new clients, that it is not easy for the consultant to estimate the amount of time that will be required to perform the study. Some allowance is usually made for this by quoting tolerances for the fee; for example, the fee is quoted at $100,000, plus or minus 15 percent.

Sometimes a monthly fee is quoted together with the number of months that it is estimated will be needed to complete the assignment. Under either arrangement the client can terminate the agreement if he or she is unhappy with the work being performed. The agreement usually requires thirty days' written notice before termination.

In spite of the difficulty of determining in advance the time an assignment will require, I would not recommend an open-ended arrangement to either a consultant or a client. It is worth taking the trouble to define an assignment carefully at the outset to avoid misunderstandings later.

One of the variables that makes fee estimation hard is the difficulty in maintaining a planned schedule of client interviews. The consultant cannot schedule time productively when the client cancels appointments or when they are difficult to arrange. Sometimes the problem is with obtaining performance reports and other data required. This information may not be as complete as necessary or may simply be unavailable, in which case the consultant must spend time developing it.

The consultant usually specifies in the letter of proposal that information required will be promptly provided and that interviews will be set up so as to make the best use of the consultant's time, giving due consideration, of course, to the schedules of company personnel. Where the client-consultant relationship is good, the consultant should be able to do an efficient job of

scheduling time. Misunderstandings usually occur when the consultant has not maintained a
close relationship with the client and where there
have been few, if any, interim reports.

When the client makes requests for services
beyond those specified in the original understanding, the consultant should determine whether
this work will require an increase in fees, and if
so, notify the client immediately in writing. One
of the frequent causes for misunderstanding is that
the consultant, flattered by the client's request,
does not consider what it involves, and does not
tell the client that it will require more time, and
hence higher fees, than previously estimated. This
results either in the consultant swallowing the
excess or in billing the client a fee higher than
anticipated. Both can cause bad feelings.

Governmental bodies and some commercial
enterprises frequently request consultants to specify
their hourly rate and the number of hours that it
is estimated will be required to complete a study.
As far as I can tell, this approach does not usually
provide any better control of the consultant's time
or produce greater efficiency than the monthly
or total fee estimate does.

In planning a study, sufficient time must be
allowed for developing findings and recommen-

dations and the production of the report. In my own experience and that of many other consulting seniors, it requires about as much time to analyze the information and develop the report as it does to secure the data. I use this as a rule of thumb in developing an estimate of fees.

The client should not expect to see the consultants on the job every day for the duration of the study, unless the report is written on the client's premises. If the subject of the study is sensitive, it is better for the consultant to prepare the report in his or her own offices, since clerical support is needed. If the client provides this, the consultant's findings may become known indiscriminately and prematurely.

Travel, clerical, and other out-of-pocket costs are usually billed separately. Sometimes the client requests an advance estimate of the cost for out-of-pocket expenses. It is not easy to calculate the exact travel and living costs that may be involved, and many firms are reluctant to provide this estimate unless a complete understanding has been reached on these matters.

I cannot emphasize too strongly that, even where the relations between the client and the consultant are excellent and of long standing, the client should be meticulous about requiring the consultant to provide an estimate of fees and to perform the study within the estimate. As previously stated, the original agreement should be supplemented by further agreements where additional work is requested. All understandings should be in writing to avoid later disputes. A consulting arrangement is a business venture and should be treated as such no matter how cordial the personal relationships may be.

Retainer Arrangements

Occasionally, a client and consultant will set up a retainer arrangement. Under this type of agreement, the client pays the consultant a monthly or annual fee for general advice and counsel. There are usually some stipulations as to the amount of the consultant's time that will be involved and when the consultant will be available. I would not recommend this approach for the performance of a specific study, but where there is a long-term relationship between the client and consultant and assistance of a generalized kind is needed, it works out satisfactorily.

Consultant vs. Employee

At first glance, it may sometimes seem that it makes better economic sense to hire another executive than to employ a consultant. For example, a consultant making $60,000 per year base salary would probably be billed to a client for a month's assignment at a fee of $18,000 to $20,000, plus out-of-pocket expenses. The company could hire a comparable employee to perform the assignment at $60,000 per year, or for a monthly cost of $5,000, to which must be added the cost of benefits—vacation, sick leave, holidays, insurance, etc.—at approximately $33\frac{1}{3}$ percent, or $1,600, for a total of $6,600 per month. Thus, there would be an apparent savings of over $13,000.

Further, there is always an element of uncertainty in dealing with a consultant, who may not be able to deliver the product or results expected. As pointed out in another section, a consultant can cause internal problems. While the methods described in this book eliminate much of the risk in using a consultant, it is still there. So why employ one?

You may need to use a consultant for reasons given in earlier chapters. There is a question as to whether a new employee can perform the assignment as well as a carefully selected consultant.

Furthermore, what are you going to do with the employee afterwards? It is not easy to terminate an employee. The employee group tends to protect each other, and they can give many reasons for retaining an employee when an assignment is completed. A client of ours, C. R. Smith, then president of American Airlines, once said to me of an employee who was no longer needed, "Every time I fire the so-and-so, I find him out behind the barn in Tulsa."

The employment of a consultant, however, is expected to end when the assignment is over. The consultant may suggest many reasons for being retained, but dismissal can be accomplished without real difficulty. It should also be taken into consideration that, since the consultant will have worked only on a specific assignment, it will be relatively easy to evaluate his or her product and costs.

Only you can decide whether it is better to use an employee or a consultant to help solve your problem. I can only suggest that all the pros and cons should be carefully considered before making a decision.

Niggardliness Can Be Self-Defeating

While a company cannot be concerned with the economic viability of a consulting firm, executives should bear in mind that it is important that topflight consultants be available to assist in solving present problems and planning future courses of action. Making life hard for them could be a mistake.

Several years ago, the leaders in the oil industry decided to eliminate their own drilling activities and use drilling contractors. In an economic pinch, the oil companies squeezed the contractors so hard that they virtually put them out of business. When the companies realized what they were doing, they changed their tactics and permitted the contractors to make a decent profit. Both the oil companies and the drilling contractors have benefited. The relationship between consultants and management is analogous. While the consultants should not gouge their clients, they must be allowed to make reasonable profits in order to provide the services that industry and government need.

The Bottom Line

In the final analysis, what the consultant is worth to you depends on what is produced. Two cases with which I am familiar will illustrate this point.

The first was that of the XYZ Company. This company was experiencing heavy losses and was deeply in debt. Management decided to employ a consulting firm that specialized in strategic planning to help it eliminate unprofitable operations and point up areas where the company should concentrate its efforts in order to improve profits quickly.

XYZ's management made its arrangements with a senior member of the consulting firm, whom they never saw again. A group of very young and inexperienced consultants was brought in to work on the project.

During the next six months, these consultants interviewed every company executive who could possibly provide them with information about the situation. They also talked with a large number of the company's creditors and others with whom it dealt. After extensive deliberation, they came up with a plan that required the company to move out of certain markets where the losses were heavy and to concentrate their efforts on more productive market areas. The plan seemed logical and XYZ's management accepted it. The consultants' fees came to over $1 million.

When management came to cost out the implementation of the plan, they discovered that they could not lessen overhead costs fast enough to accommodate the reduced size of the company. There did not seem to be any way for them to get from where they were to where the consultant recommended that they go. They were forced to shelve the recommendations, and narrowly averted bankruptcy by selling one of the company's divisions.

The second example illustrates a diametrically opposite situation. It concerned a manufacturer of parts for the aviation and automobile industries that had just undertaken a major contract for a branch of the federal government. Management had some questions about the efficiency of the company's operations and retained a consultant to do a general survey of its four divisions.

The consultant began by visiting the division charged with carrying out the government contract and discovered that the situation was much worse than top management had realized. To begin with, the general manager of the division was an alcoholic who began drinking in the morning and was completely useless by afternoon. Some of the work methods were inefficient and the plant was unclean. Many workers were idle.

More importantly, the consultant made a quick examination of the contract with the government and concluded that, with the company's present wages and level of productivity, fulfilling the contract would cause the company to lose many millions of dollars and wind up bankrupt.

A hurried visit by the consultant to corporate headquarters to inform the chief executive of the situation resulted in a request for the consultant to make a more detailed examination.

The thorough study that followed confirmed the original evaluation.

The company was in a dilemma. Could they get the government to alter the terms of the contract, and if not, what could they do? The consultant suggested that they open discussions with a company paying lower wage rates to see whether it would be willing to undertake the task to fulfill the contract.

Company executives first talked with government officials, who refused to release them from the contract. They then, with the help of the consultant, sought a possible partner. The consultant identified a company with lower wage rates and a more efficient operation that was willing to undertake the contract on the original terms. Appropriate arrangements were made and the consultant's client avoided bankruptcy. The consultant's fee was $30,000 for this part of the assignment.

These two examples are extreme cases. In the first, even if the consultant had charged only a dollar a day, it would have been too much from the company's point of view, since the consultant's recommendations turned out to be useless. In the second, almost any fee up to the total value of the company the consultant saved would have been a bargain. Most consulting assignments are not so easy to evaluate, but in any event, it is the results, and not the daily rate, that matter.

CHAPTER

4

DO YOU NEED A CONSULTANT?

IF SO, WHAT TYPE, AND HOW CAN YOU FIND ONE?

If business conditions, internal and external, did not change almost from day to day, life would be easier for executives and there would be little need for consultants. But executives are practically never able to sit back and relax. Either the company has a new situation to meet now, or a challenge is looming in the future. It is to deal with problems of change that the consultant may be called in.

Perhaps sales volume isn't growing, or the company is losing market share, or profit ratios are declining, or the quality of the product is deteriorating. Possibly the company has what might be called a happy problem: its products are selling so well that it will need to increase its manufacturing capability, or find new areas in which to invest. Or management foresees that a problem will arise later: a strong executive is about to retire, or an aggressive competitor has appeared on the scene, or staff is multiplying, or union demands are becoming more pressing.

However, if it is true that consultants are only needed where there is a problem, it does not follow that every problem requires a consultant to solve it. Many problems can be dealt with more quickly and efficiently by company management than by an outsider; others are very difficult to handle without outside assistance. If you are considering the use of a consultant, it is wise to begin by making sure that your problem falls into the second group.

I recently conducted an informal poll of a dozen or so top-level executives to find out whether and under what circumstances they were accustomed to using consultants. Since they were friends or acquaintances of mine, it will probably surprise no one to learn that they all endorsed the employment of consultants, although one of them, an extremely capable and successful executive, had reservations. This executive, who asked not to be quoted by name, maintained that "too many people use too many consultants. The use of consultants is too often what I call the 'lazy man's way'—in effect, an opportunity to let someone else do work which people in the company could do if properly motivated and/or properly led." Still, he said that he did use consultants on specialized projects for which his company was not equipped, and also "very occasionally, for corroborative purposes—that is, to test internal conclusions when the consequences of making a mistake would be severe."

Almost all the respondents stated that they regularly used consultants for specialized studies of one sort or another and occasionally for more generalized assignments. Otherwise, there was considerable variation in the purposes for which they had recently sought a consultant's help. Among the areas mentioned, in descending order of frequency, were various types of compensation and benefit studies, marketing and market research studies, strategic planning, organization planning, financial analysis, executive search, and mergers and consolidations.

Obviously, there is no simple, foolproof method for determining whether you should engage a consultant. If you are thinking of doing so, I suggest that you begin by defining your problem and its ramifications and making a preliminary analysis of its probable cause. This definition and analysis should involve a reasonably thorough study of the situation. Although shooting from the hip can have its uses, there are many dangers in rushing to solve a problem without being sure what it is. You will find this preliminary work particularly worthwhile if you eventually decide to bring in a consultant. A capable consultant who knows what you need can usually get results for you; a consultant who is working on the wrong problem may waste a considerable amount of time and money.

You will probably want to discuss the problem with the executive in charge of the problem area, who in turn may discuss it with his or her personal staff, and perhaps hold meetings with lower-level executives. When the analysis is completed, you will find it helpful to state your findings in writing. Reducing the problem to written form will clarify your thinking and help to ensure that you ask yourself the right questions.

It is possible that you will have found the solution of the problem yourself in the course of the analysis. If not, the time has come to ask yourself whether outside help is needed. Does the company have the resources to develop the solution in-house? Or is it best to use a consultant, and if so, what type?

When to Use a Consultant

Of course, each situation is different. But there are several factors that are almost always important in deciding whether the use of a consultant is desirable.

The Availability of Company Staff and Their Competence in the Problem Area. As a rule, company staff is already employed in activities important to the company. In determining whether to use in-house staff or a consultant, consider what would be involved in diverting the staff's attention to solving a new and difficult problem situation. Will they be able to give it the time needed? Will they undertake the new project willingly or will they believe their present assignments are more important? The competence of company staff is relatively easy to assess on the basis of their background, training, and experience. If they lack the necessary expertise, or are not available for the project, you almost certainly need a consultant.

The Importance and Urgency of the Solution. When the solution of the problem may be critical to the company's success, or when quick results are urgently needed, you may prefer to use a consultant with in-depth skills in the problem area who is free from other responsibilities and can devote full time to the project.

The Political Dimensions of the Problem. When the causes of the problem are controversial and internal politics are involved, you may hesitate to use internal staff because taking part in the dispute might impair their future effectiveness. Also, it is questionable whether internal staff can be completely objective in such situations.

The Confidentiality of the Matters Involved. The use of a consultant is usually desirable when the information and recommendations to be developed are of a confidential nature. Projects that are likely to involve confidential material include: developing top management compensation plans, formulating management personnel contracts, financial studies, evaluating proposed acquisitions, merger studies, studies involving or authorized by the board of directors, organization studies, and management succession plans.

Narrowing the Field

If you decide that the problem does in fact require the services of a consultant, the next question is, what *type* would be most helpful— a generalist or a specialist, a large firm or a single individual, a national firm, a regional firm, or a foreign firm?

Does the problem concern the performance of one activity in a single department? Can it be described as a sales problem, a manufacturing difficulty, a materiel management problem, or something similar? If so, a specialist in the problem area would be a likely candidate.

If the problem is difficult to define and/or seems to have its roots in several departments, you would probably be wise to engage a generalist. For example, a problem involving inadequate marketing results that lead to a decline in profits could also be related to manufacturing performance, or perhaps to a failure on the part of the Finance Department to exercise proper cost control. This sort of problem requires a multidimensional study, for which a general management consultant is better equipped than a specialist.

A reputable general management firm is usually a good choice for important, confidential studies that will require the approval of the board of directors. The recommendations of such firms, which are accustomed to taking the top management point of view, are likely to carry considerable weight. Overall organization studies, strategic planning studies, and top management succession studies fall into this group. More technical, less significant confidential studies, in the personnel or financial areas, for example, may be better accomplished by specialists.

When there is a present or anticipated vacancy in an executive position and no suitable candidate is available in-house, an executive search firm is the obvious answer.

Case Histories

The cases described in the following pages give some idea of the kind of problems management faces in choosing a consultant. These cases are composites of a number of situations with which I am familiar, although of course none is an actual client case. They demonstrate management's thought processes in determining the type of expertise needed, the decisions reached, and the results.

They also illustrate various situations in which the services of a consultant may be required, including: company staff not available or not qualified in the problem area, an important and urgent problem requiring a quick solution, a problem with political dimensions, a confidential situation, and a need to replace an executive. The last case shows the result when the problem was not correctly diagnosed by the company and the wrong type of consultant was used.

1. *The case of conflicting departmental goals where company staff was not qualified to solve the*

problem. Solved by a general management consultant.

This case involves a situation where the problems in the manufacturing operation could have been heavily influenced by two other departments, marketing and finance. The problem was resolved by a general management consultant familiar with all three functions.

The maker of hand tools and oil field equipment had a problem. The Manufacturing Department was not meeting its production forecast and was not operating within approved budget levels. The vice president for manufacturing, who had not participated in the early stages of the annual plan development, had agreed only with considerable reluctance to production and cost targets set by marketing and finance. The production forecast was tailored to conform with the marketing forecast. The cost budget originally developed by manufacturing had been modified under pressure from finance to meet financial goals. The vice president–manufacturing had told the executive group that he believed the company needed a new plant and equipment.

The president pondered the problem and asked himself these questions:

a. Was the vice president–manufacturing unduly pressured in forecasting production and cost levels?

b. Is the vice president–manufacturing competent?

c. Does the company really need a new plant or new equipment?

d. Are the present manufacturing methods suitable and up-to-date?

The president noted that the manufacturing staff had not been able to solve the problem, although they had been working on it for some time. He had these questions about his best course of action:

a. Should the company bring in a new executive to head manufacturing and let him or her resolve the problem? Would this be fair in view of the vice president–manufacturing's strenuous objections to the targets established for his department?

b. Should the company employ a manufacturing consultant to identify the causes of the problem and develop a solution?

c. Since several departments were involved, should the company bring in a general management consultant for the same purpose?

The president believed that it would be only fair to bring in a general management consultant to evaluate the situation and make an objective determination on the questions raised. He concluded that a specialist in manufacturing might not give proper consideration to the positions of marketing and finance.

The consultant, after an in-depth study of the situation, reported that a new plant was not needed, but that some equipment should be replaced. He found that the methods used were generally suitable. He recommended that the Manufacturing Department be brought into the planning cycle at the beginning of the development of the annual plan, so that they would not be required to react to targets already established by others.

His recommendations were adopted. Positive results were not quickly achieved, but after the new equipment was installed, the production capability improved and targets began to be met. The introduction of manufacturing into its proper place in the planning cycle resulted in improvements in the product and had a favorable impact on company efficiency and cost.

2. *The case of a company with numerous problems requiring prioritizing and solved by the use of specialized consulting services—an urgent problem requiring a quick solution.*

This company, a producer and distributor of baked goods, was heavily dependent domestically on two product lines. It had been unsuccessful in efforts to introduce new products. Its growth rate was stagnant, and its profits were declining.

The company's profitability was significantly affected by the operations of the five large regional distributors it owned. These distributors produced, sold, and distributed the company's baked goods over wide areas. Their costs were much higher than those of six independent distributors with which the company also worked.

The company's International Division earned good profits. However, its earnings accounted for only 10 percent of company results. The company was selling its products in only three foreign markets.

A new company president had recently been appointed.

He believed the following:

a. The company must reduce the costs of the company-owned distributors or sell them. This problem was serious and required a fast answer. Management was reluctant to part with the distributors because they gave the company better control over the markets they served.

b. The company should add new product lines in the United States. At issue was, what products should be introduced and how much would it cost to launch them? In this process, how could the company avoid repeating previous failures?

c. It was questionable whether the present vice president—marketing should be retained.

d. International markets appeared to offer opportunities for growth and profits. But to which countries should the company expand? With what products?

The president believed that he must find the answers to these problems quickly. He felt that consulting services might be helpful, but what type or types? A cost-reduction specialist? A specialist in distribution? A domestic marketing consultant? An international marketing consultant? A general management consultant with expertise in many areas?

Would work in one problem area provide knowledge valuable for solving problems in other areas? Should the company tackle its problems one at a time or simultaneously?

The president decided that he must prioritize the problems and attack the most serious first. He believed that the most urgent of the problems was cost reduction of the company-owned distributors and, therefore, retained a consulting firm that specialized in manufacturing and distribution. They found that corporate headquarters was requiring field personnel to submit voluminous and often unnecessary reports. They developed a simple reporting system that permitted eliminating a large number of clerical personnel. At the same time, the consultants made recommendations for the routing of trucks that permitted greater route coverage with fewer trucks. They increased the role of the drivers to provide improved service to retailers. The result was that the cost of operating company distributors came close to that of the independents and sales and service improved.

To deal with the company's marketing problems, the president hired a new domestic marketing vice president and a new head for the International Division. The new international executive moved the company into a number of foreign markets with its existing products and some new ones. The products were well received and the operations soon became profitable.

The new vice president–marketing for domestic operations was not successful in introducing new products. He did, however, manage to increase the market share of the company's existing products, with a favorable effect on growth and profitability.

These successful results involved attacking problems one at a time, in order of priority, using specialized consulting services.

3. *The case of a company that had problems in all areas and where a new president resolved them with the help of a general management consultant.*

This company, a large service business, was suffering from a general malaise. To begin with, its products were undependable; their quality level was below that of competitive products, and their costs were higher.

The field organization responsible for providing and selling the product was divided into several units reporting separately to corporate headquarters. It was difficult to coordinate sales and service at the local level or to fix responsibility for results. The company lacked the tools to measure the quality of its products and the cost of providing them. Its debt burden was large. Seasoned and strong corporate executives had recently retired; most of those remaining seemed ineffective.

A new chief executive was brought in from outside. He asked himself these questions:

a. Should he bring in replacements for weak corporate staff members and let the new appointees take actions to strengthen their respective departments?

b. Would this be sufficient? The present alignment of duties and responsibilities seemed illogical. Strengthening the present organization units might not solve the problems.

c. Would that approach get results quickly enough in view of the company's serious condition?

d. Should the company bring in a consultant?

e. If so, should it be a general management consultant, a specialist in each problem area, an industry generalist, or several industry specialists?

f. Could specialists help to create a homogeneous, well-balanced organization?

The president elected to retain a general management consultant, giving him these assignments: first, to attack the basic problem and develop a new plan of organization with fewer levels that would strengthen the company's capabilities for providing and selling its products; and second, to look for cost-reduction opportunities.

The consultant, working with a study team of company executives, developed a streamlined organization structure and identified opportunities for reducing costs. The five large regional line and staff departments in the field were abolished, eliminating approximately seven hundred employees. Staff support to the field was to be

provided by corporate staff that would not need
to have its numbers increased.

Corporate line direction was to be provided by
five regional vice presidents located at corporate
headquarters who would use existing corporate
staff as their support to the field. In the field a
manager was to be appointed for each geographic
location. Local staff was regrouped to support and
report to the local manager. This resulted in a
reduction of an additional two hundred field employees. The chief executive approved the plan
and asked the consultant to assist in installing it.

Working with the same management team and
with the support of the president, the consultant
held work sessions with key personnel from each
department to be sure they understood their role
in the new organization and how they would
function in the new environment. He also wanted
to secure their agreement on cost-reduction opportunities and develop a timetable for action.
Within two years the company was making a
vigorous comeback and is today a leader in its
industry.

4. *The case of a politically sensitive problem in a*
   company needing new directions and a new
   marketing strategy. Solved by the use of a spe-

*cialist in strategic planning who recommended
an acceptable course of action.*

This consumer products company was experiencing declining profits and zero growth. Its
product lines were mature. It had not made a
successful new product introduction in years; its
principal competitor had done well with a number of new products and had far outpaced it in
both growth and profits.

A veteran, entrenched chairman and chief executive officer had never permitted the reduction
of present profits in order to introduce new lines.
He exercised tight control over marketing and
advertising plans, which had to be approved not
only by him but also by his wife, a person with
no business background.

Under pressure from the board, he had recently promoted the head of the International
Division to the post of president and chief operating officer.

The new president was aware of the problems
and thought he knew their causes. He asked
himself:

a. Could he make the necessary investments
in new products and carry out other needed
changes and still hold his position?

b. Could he convince the chairman of the need for these changes? Or would he simply find himself discredited by the chairman, as many of his predecessors had been?

c. Should he recommend acquiring another company in the hope of diluting the chairman's authority?

d. Should he bring in a consultant with a reputation for sound strategic planning and let the consultant recommend a course of action? Would a strategic planner be able to suggest moves that would put the company ahead of competition?

e. Should he bring in a general management consultant who might suggest the actions needed to meet present competitive thrusts?

f. Should he take it in stages, first bringing in a generalist and keeping the use of a strategic planning specialist in reserve for use if necessary?

The president believed that going over the chairman's head to the board would be disloyal. He felt that he must make the necessary decisions himself. He eventually concluded that bringing in a strategic planning consultant would be the most fruitful course of action.

The consultant recommended leapfrogging the competition by acquiring new products through the purchase of companies that produced items the company could market through its existing channels.

Since this recommendation did not embarrass the chairman, it was accepted and put into effect, with good results.

5. *The case of an important executive vacancy solved by the use of an executive search firm*

The president realized that he must replace the present marketing vice president, who was nearing retirement.

Working under the vice president–marketing were a number of marketing specialists, each responsible for a defined area: advertising and promotion, pricing, sales, distribution, planning, etc. None had overall marketing experience. Questions:

a. Should the company select the present staff member who appears to have the greatest

potential and train that person in the phases
of marketing with which he or she is unfamiliar?

b. Or should the company go outside to obtain an experienced marketing executive? If
so, how will the outsider be received by the
inside contenders? Can anything be done
to minimize the risk of insider resentment?
Or is the need for a proven executive so great
that the risk is worth taking?

c. If the company decides to bring in new talent, should it use an executive search firm
or do the search in-house?

The president decided to bring in someone from
outside. Through an executive search firm, the
company found an executive with expertise in
marketing many different types of products similar to those of the company, familiar with company channels of distribution, and who had
several years of successful experience as vice
president of marketing of a company in a related
industry.

When his appointment was announced, the
company lost one of its marketing specialists, who,
fortunately, was replaceable from within. The

others accepted the sound leadership and fresh approaches supplied by the new vice president.

6. *The case of a failure to identify the problem, the use of the wrong consultant, and the consequences*

This case illustrates the damage that can be caused by not identifying the real problem and by selecting the wrong type of consultant—one who makes the situation worse by taking a destructive approach.

At the time the trouble began, the company was a diversified organization with ten profit-centered divisions, each of which handled different types of consumer products. Each division was headed by a president, supported by competent divisional staff, and held accountable for annual results.

The central corporate staff was small, heavily oriented toward financial planning and cost control.

With the chairman, the staff reviewed the annual division plans. Once the plans had been approved, each divisional president was authorized to manage as he wished consistent with the plan.

Under this approach the company's growth and profits were increasing at a rate that commanded the respect of the financial community.

The division heads and some members of corporate staff began to question whether the company was investing sufficiently in the future. They wished to develop and promote new products and/or possibly acquire other companies with needed products. The chairman felt strongly that this was not a problem and in turn questioned the capabilities of the executives who offered the criticism. Feeling that he must deal with the suggestion that all was not well, he was torn between (1) hiring a strategic planning consultant who could evaluate the company's commitments to the future, or (2) bringing in a specialist to evaluate the performance and capabilities of company executives.

He chose the latter course. Unfortunately, the consultant he selected concentrated on the weaknesses of the executives and on their opinions of the chairman. He demoralized the staff by telling each of the incompetencies of the others.

The chairman dismissed the consultant within days after he had given his first report, but by then the damage had been done. The chairman lost confidence in his division executives, and one by one they resigned or were discharged. The chairman and the corporate staff began to take over responsibility for division profits and growth. The number of corporate staff members increased dramatically as division profits plummeted. Within a few years this former industry leader faced declining profits and a low growth rate.

Summary

These cases are intended to give some idea of the type of situation in which a consultant may be needed. They also illustrate the questions that face management in determining what type of consultant to employ. The last case demonstrates the unfortunate results that can come of judgmental errors in defining the problem and in the selection process.

Finding Suitable Consultants

Given the large number of firms and individuals practicing consulting and the absence of a central information center, determining which among them has the required qualifications is not easy. There are, however, several sources to which a potential client can turn for information.

One notable resource is ACME, Inc., the Association of Management Consulting Firms, 230 Park Avenue, New York, N.Y. 10017. While ACME has an accredited membership of only 62 of the estimated 3,500 consulting firms, it keeps on file the names and addresses of approximately 2,000 firms along with some information about their practice areas. (ACME has listed 803 areas of specialty, both by function and by industry.) Recently, two of the large accounting firms' consulting groups with about 7,500 consultants have been accepted into ACME. We understand that the consulting groups of other large accounting firms are planning to apply for membership. This will enhance the size and importance of ACME dramatically. Officially, ACME only provides information on the capabilities and areas of competence of member firms; yet, it will make available any data it may have on nonmember firms.

Another potential source of information is the Institute of Management Consultants, or IMC, whose headquarters are also in New York City, at 19 West 44th Street, New York, N.Y. 10036. IMC accredits individual consultants on the basis of written and oral examinations and on past performance. Those approved by the Institute may use the appellation C.M.C. (Certified Management Consultant) after their names. The Institute will supply names of C.M.C.'s, the firms in which they are employed, and their areas of specialty. It does not offer information on the capabilities of the consulting firms represented, although the quality of the firm is looked at when the individual consultant is accredited. Only 1,600 consultants have been designated C.M.C.'s by the IMC as of late 1984.

Nonaffiliation with these organizations is not necessarily a bad sign. Many highly qualified and competent consultants are not members of IMC. As previously stated, ACME represents a relatively small number of firms; many of the largest are not members.

Another potential source of information is AMC (Association of Management Consultants), 500 N. Michigan Avenue, Suite 1400, Chicago, Ill. 60611. While their members are mostly smaller firms, AMC has a reputation for high membership standards.

The American Institute of Certified Public Accountants, 1211 Avenue of the Americas, New York, N.Y. 10036, will provide information about the types of consulting services provided by its member firms, primarily the "Big Eight."

The accounting firms generate by far the largest volume of consulting practice. Some question their ability to be objective in situations that might affect their relationships with major audit clients. If such a disability does exist, nevertheless, there are many situations where it would not pose a problem.

In spite of commanding the lion's share of the U.S. consulting practice, in my opinion, none of the accounting firms has gained preeminence, in the consulting field, as have McKinsey & Co., Booz Allen & Hamilton, Arthur D. Little, the Boston Consulting Group, Harbridge House, and others. However, they should not be overlooked as a source; their ranks include many distinguished practitioners.

To locate an executive search firm, a logical source is the Association of Executive Search Consultants, 151 Railroad Avenue, Greenwich, Conn. 06830. This association represents only a small percentage of the total number of search firms. Any member firm will undoubtedly be reputable, since the association requires that its members conform to high ethical standards. Other executive search firms, many highly qualified, can be found by consulting the yellow pages. Also, some general management consultants provide executive search assistance.

Business friends are another valuable source of information. They can tell you in what types of situation they have brought in consultants, and provide evaluations of the contributions and competence of individuals and firms.

Banks and other lending institutions are also good sources. They probably have employed consultants for internal studies and will have observed the use of consultants by bank clients. In the latter case their knowledge may be second-hand but still valuable. Financial institutions should be objective and able to provide sound information.

For companies that operate in Great Britain, the Institute of Management Consultants in Great Britain maintains a management consultant registry containing information on consultants and consulting firms in that country. They are located at Alfred House, 22–24 Cromwell Place, London SW7 LGI.

In most foreign countries there are branches of U.S. banks that can provide information on local consulting firms. Where there is a large American population, there is usually a U.S.

Chamber of Commerce for the country. They, too, will probably have information on consulting firms.

Conclusion

This section has provided some information about how to locate the type of consultant and/or consulting firm needed. But it must be recalled that determining your problem is the first step. Now you are in a position to choose a consultant of the type needed. The actual selection of the consultant will be discussed in the next chapter.

CHAPTER

5

SELECTING
YOUR
CONSULTANT

You are now ready to select your consultant. You have defined the problem and its causes. You have evaluated your internal situation and determined that you need to go outside for consulting assistance. You have determined the type of consultant or consultants that would be most suitable for your needs. If your company has several problems, you have decided which ones you want the consultant to work on and the order of priority.

You will want to give the selection of a consultant your careful attention. The choice you make is likely to have an important effect on your company's future, not to mention your own.

Identifying Prospective Consultants

When you have determined what it is that you want the consultant to do, you are ready to begin the selection process. The methods outlined earlier will enable you to make up a list of consultants who might be suitable. This done, it will be useful to obtain their brochures or any other information available on their past performance and areas of expertise. You may wish to contact possible candidates directly and ask them for additional information about their capabilities, the types of clients that they serve, the kinds of situations in which they are most commonly involved, and any other information that would be helpful to you in deciding which ones you will wish to consider further. In this way you may develop a short list of several promising candidates.

Very frequently the consultant will seek out the client. A consultant will identify prospective clients, secure available information about them, and try to arrange meetings, either through common acquaintances or friends or directly. The process of determining whether such a consultant is the one you need is the same as if you had initiated the action.

Selecting the Consultant Is a Personal Decision

While the consultant is employed to serve the company's interests, selecting the consultant is a personal decision for the executive who employs him or her. The two will be working together for a considerable period of time, and the association is more productive when there is mutual liking and respect. It goes without saying that the consultant should have the qualifications to perform the assignment; it is also important that he or she have a personality that is pleasing to you.

In the words of Edgar Cullman, the chairman of Culbro, "Before taking on a consultant, one would have to be prepared to share with them all the thoughts, problems, and opportunities inherent in the situation about which they are consulting. It is very important that the consultant be given wholehearted cooperation in order to be able to give thoughtful conclusions. You cannot use a consultant when holding one hand behind you." This being true, as I believe it is, you will not want to engage a consultant about whom you have reservations.

Your estimate of how the consultant will work with your other executives and lower-level employees is another important consideration in your selection. Bear in mind that a tactless, insensitive consultant can weaken the company members' faith in one another, with a disastrous effect on morale.

Planning the Interview

When you have reduced the candidate list to a manageable number, you will want to arrange interviews with the prospects. The best results will be secured by preplanning these discussions.

You will want to provide a comfortable meeting room for interviewing the candidates, as pleasant and as free from disturbance as possible. You should arrange to avoid interruptions during the meetings.

Allow ample time for the meeting. It will take you a little time for preliminaries and to set the stage for the interview. It is difficult to determine exactly how much time will be required, but, depending on the nature of the problem, between one and two hours should be adequate. There should be no rushing on the part of either the client or the consultant.

You will try to give the consultant a favorable opinion of you and your company. The consultant's opinion of the client will influence his or her dedication if selected. The old truism that man does not live by bread alone applies particularly to the client-consultant relationship. Allow time to listen to the consultant and answer questions, so that the consultant will know that you value his or her opinion.

Plan to describe your problem in such a way that you let the consultant know that you consider the matter, and the selection of the right consultant, to be important. This will dignify the situation and increase the consultant's interest in working on the assignment.

Conducting the Interview

You are now ready to conduct the meetings with your prospects. Appointments have been set up, and you are about to sit down with a consultant.

It will be helpful if you first put the consultant at ease so that he or she will talk freely and give you the kind of information needed. I have found that it is wise to begin the meeting with some pleasantries that do not involve the subject matter for which the meeting was called. When both parties have relaxed, progress will be much faster. You, of course, want to form an idea of what the consultant is like, so putting him or her at ease creates an environment that is productive for you.

Describe the problem fully. After the initial pleasantries, it is wise for the client to set the stage by describing the problem and its causes in some detail. This should include describing the environment in which the problem arose and the people who have some responsibility for the problem areas. Remember that the consultant is unfamiliar with your company. Sometimes the client's description of the situation is cryptic and couched in language peculiar to the company's business, making it difficult for the consultant to understand the problem. The consultant is thus unable to make a suitable proposal.

Sometimes, too, the client does not want to reveal the magnitude of the problem. This gives the consultant a misleading impression. The consultant will need all the information available about the problem, what you want done, and the product you expect.

You will want to invite questions from the consultant. These questions will provide a good indication as to whether the person is qualified. Are the questions pertinent, or did the consultant go off on a tangent into areas that are not important to the situation under consideration? Do the questions indicate prior experience and knowledge in the problem area? One can usually tell by the type of question asked whether the consultant has worked in a similar situation and is familiar with the type of problem requiring study.

Observe the consultant's attitude. Certain consultants tend not to pay close attention to what the client says. They look around the room and not at the client when he or she is speaking. They appear to have fastened their interest on some activity outside the window, or are looking around to see what objects of interest may be found inside. When questioned, such a consultant seems to have not fully heard the description of the situation and does not understand the problem. If you encounter such a person, it is best to terminate the interview and give the consultant no further consideration.

Secure specific information about the consultant's background. You will wish to question the consultant about any prior experience with similar situations. Or, is there anything in the person's educational background that would be helpful in solving the problem? Sometimes the consultant will not have had any experience directly related to the client situation, but will have dealt with situations related in some way.

Learn the consultant's approach to the problem. You will want to know how this person expects to attack it, what information will be required, and from what sources. Will it be obtained from interviews, or can a great deal of it be obtained from records and reports? Whom will the consultant want to see? What data will be needed?

Very often it is wise to have a company study team work with the consultant. In this way the study team will become knowledgeable about the problem and what is important to its solution. The team can be of great assistance in helping to implement the eventual recommendations. If you and the consultant intend to use a study team, you would wish to know how it would be employed. It is best to assign the consultant to direct the study team, and an experienced consultant should insist upon this.

The consultant will indicate whether he or she has worked with study teams before and on what basis, and will give an opinion on whether the use of a study team on your project will be advisable. This may be an influencing factor in your decision.

Sometimes, of course, the problem may be of such a nature that you do not wish company employees to work with the consultant. This would be true when the study involves a political problem or a subject that is highly confidential.

Learn which consultants will be assigned to the project. Sometimes the consultant will expect to use one or more associates in the work on your assignment. If so, it will be important for you to obtain their experience and qualifications. If their backgrounds appear to be suitable, you will wish to interview them personally to learn whether you find them qualified and whether their personalities are conducive to good working relationships.

Learn who will be responsible for directing the study. You will want to know whether the consultant first interviewed will be working on the study, and if so, what that person's role will be. A frequently heard complaint is "I never saw the consultant I hired after our first meeting." This sometimes happens because consulting firms are inclined to use consultants who are good salesmen to develop new business. The sales consultant does not always work on the study itself. However, if you have made your arrangement with a specific consultant, you may want that individual to be personally involved, at least to the extent of being held responsible for the success of the study. At a minimum, you will want to personally interview and approve the person who will direct the actual study and those who will work on it.

Developing Your Personal Evaluation of the Consultant

In addition to the professional capabilities of the consultant, your evaluation of personality and appearance is important. Was the consultant's manner and appearance that of a professional? Does the person behave with dignity? Does the consultant look like a professional?

In recent years, the standards for professional appearance have changed somewhat. I personally prefer a consultant who is clean-shaven if male and who is neatly and appropriately dressed. Old fashioned? Yes, but if the consultant has the appearance of a professional, your employees may have a more favorable reaction.

Did the consultant seem at ease or nervous during the interview? Was the person fidgety, or relaxed and able to behave in an easy and likable way? You will wish to evaluate how the consultant displayed knowledge. Did the individual seem arrogant, appearing to feel superior because of what he or she knew? Or was conversation matter-of-fact, providing an easy exchange of information without arrogance?

You will wish to consider whether the consultant showed enthusiasm about the project. Sometimes a consultant seems to be so blasé that he doesn't seem to care whether he or she works on a project or not. This is not conducive to a good working relationship. An eagerness to develop the solution to the problem is a real asset.

Did the consultant use simple, understandable language, or rely heavily on "consultese," the language of consultants? There are so many "in" words used by consultants that it is sometimes difficult for the "common man" to understand what they are saying. Never hesitate to ask for an explanation of any term with which you are not familiar. I do not particularly like consultants or others who rely on this "in" language. It seems to convey that they feel that, because they know these words, they are superior to the average individual. Or it may mask a feeling of inferiority. Neither attitude is desirable.

A closely related question is, was the consultant pompous? Did the person seem down-to-earth, or appear to hold himself or herself above the common herd? Most employees don't like to work with pompous consultants.

Is there anything about the consultant that irritates you personally? We once had a client who was unable to feel confidence in short people. If you have a prejudice of this kind, it is probably useless to try and fight against it.

A good indication of the probable reaction of your employees to the consultant is the opinion of your receptionist and secretary. When the consultant was in the waiting room, did he or she request favors from the receptionist? Did the consultant act toward him or her in a friendly way? Was the individual fatuous or overly gracious? What was the receptionist's reaction to the consultant? Your secretary, who has usually set up the meeting and shown the consultant in, can provide information on how the person behaved toward her or him. In a number of instances, secretaries have influenced a decision unfavorably because the consultant acted overly friendly, asked too many favors, or was arrogant.

The opinions of your executives are important. Very frequently clients arrange for consultants to meet with several executives, perhaps including those with whom the consultant will work. It is best to remember, however, that some of them may not wish a consultant to be brought in to deal with this problem or may be prejudiced against their use in general.

Does the consultant appear action-oriented? Could this person help you get results? Sometimes consultants are concerned primarily with securing information, not with using it to arrive at conclusions and recommendations that will achieve your goals. It is of no value to have unused "black books" from consultants in your desk drawer. You are concerned with getting appropriate action. The right consultant can be of great help in this regard.

The interviewing and evaluation process should weed out those not qualified and provide you with one or more suitable candidates.

Checking Out the References of the Consultant

Why You Need to Check Consultants' References. It is well to check the consultant's references thoroughly before employing the person. An impressive manner, a pleasing personality, and a well-printed brochure are not always reliable indications of ability. Most of us place too much emphasis on appearance and manner. We need to obtain information on the consultant's past performance with clients before a final selection is made.

There are many consultants who really apply themselves, have all the needed qualifications, and do an excellent job for the client. There are others who do not. They may not have the qualifications, or they may not apply themselves.

Some may work well on certain types of assignments, but fail on others. Some may be excellent in developing background information, but do a poor job in analyzing it and using it to develop recommendations and a plan of action.

Remember that anyone who can have cards printed can become an instant consultant. Many retirees and other executives think they would like to be consultants, but not all executives make good consultants (and vice versa). An executive may be knowledgeable about the problem and even its solution, but not know how to work in a client-consultant relationship, or how to get action as a consultant.

Method of Checking References. Former clients or employers are reluctant to provide derogatory information in writing about a consultant's (or former employee's) past record. The liability for misrepresentation is too great and most are not willing to chance it.

For this reason, it is far better to obtain performance data from former clients or others by personal interview. Sitting down face-to-face with a former client usually results in a friendly atmosphere in which full information will come to light. You can describe your own situation better and get more valuable information about the former client's experience with the consultant in a personal meeting. Most businesspeople are willing to spare a few minutes for this purpose and will be helpful and informative in a face-to-face meeting.

Second best is by telephone. Here you should give the former client the opportunity to call you back to verify your identity. If your company is not well known to the person, briefly explain your business before describing your problem. The telephone interview will probably be shorter than a personal visit, so you will want to trim your interrogation to the most critical points.

Finally, you may have to write to some former clients not readily available by telephone or for a personal visit.

Types of Information Needed
in the Reference Check

Description of the kind of situation in which the consultant worked. How recent was it?

What were the results? Were the recommendations put into effect?

Did they prove sound? If not, why not?

Did the consultant address the problem for which he or she was employed?

Did the consultant perform the study within time and fee estimates?

If there was an overrun, did you agree with it before the added expense was incurred?

Did the consultant work well with company employees?

What do you consider the consultant's principal strengths? Greatest weaknesses?

Would you use the consultant again?

Sometimes the nature of the problem or a lack of time may prevent a lengthy investigation.

Nevertheless, whatever checks are possible should be made before employing any consultant.

Secure a Letter of Proposal

If you believe that the consultant has the qualifications you desire and is the type of person with whom you would wish to work, you will ask for a letter of proposal. The proposal should cover the objectives of the study, the product, the consultant's approach to the study, who will be employed on the study, who will manage the study and be responsible for results, and an estimate of time and fees.

This letter will provide another basis for confirming your judgment of the consultant. You will also want to consider the reasonableness of the professional fees, time required, and out-of-pocket expenses.

Once the letter is received you will have all the information important to the final selection: the formal proposal; the consultant's technical experience, education, and capabilities as revealed by an interview; the consultant's experience with other clients; and your personal evaluation.

When there are several contenders for the assignment, all possessing relatively equal capabilities, and their estimates of time and fees are reasonable, the decision is largely personal. Choose the one you like best.

Some consultants will not enter a competition for an assignment. If you believe such a consultant may be the one you want, put the person through the process outlined above, but more thoroughly, with the understanding that if you are satisfied by your findings and are quoted a reasonable time and fee estimate, this individual will be retained and no others will be interviewed.

The Formal Agreement

When you have chosen the consultant with whom you wish to work, be sure that both of you understand and agree upon what the person is to do, and that this agreement is fully covered in writing. If you have discussed the letter of proposal and agreed orally on changes or additions, these points should be covered in a letter from the client or in a revision of the proposal. Reducing the whole agreement to written form at the outset should go a long way toward eliminating any future differences of opinion about the scope and nature of the work to be done and the product to be developed by the consultant.

CHAPTER

6

PROVIDING FOR EMPLOYEE COOPERATION

I f you are the responsible executive in a company that has decided to bring in a consultant, it is vital that you prepare the employees to cooperate before the consultant arrives to begin work. It may seem that such preparation should be unnecessary; after all, you, the consultant, and the employees all want the company's success, so what is there to worry about? Bear in mind, however, that when you bring the consultant in, you will be more or less in the position of a doctor administering a promising new drug to a favorite patient. You have every hope that the treatment will be successful, but you must watch out for side effects. One of the commonest side effects of the appearance of consultants in a company is a certain degree of employee concern.

At minimum, employees are curious when they learn that a consultant is coming. They want to know what the person will be doing and why it was necessary to bring him or her in. Sometimes they are resentful. "We know how to run our business," they may say. "What can a consultant tell us? They only give us back what we tell them."

Some are fearful of consultants. They have known or heard of situations where, as a result of consultants' recommendations, friends have lost their jobs. This fear can have a detrimental impact on the employees' performance. Also, it can lead some employees to seek positions elsewhere—often employees that the company particularly wants to keep.

The extent of employee concern depends largely on three factors: the company's ethos and culture, the company's situation, and the nature of the consultant's study.

Company Ethos and Culture

Company atmospheres vary considerably. Certain managements, to the extent that economic circumstances permit, develop an environment or culture that takes care of its employees, provides training for their development, makes most or all of its promotions from within, and has little turnover. When it is necessary to reduce the number of employees, such managements try to do it by attrition. When dismissals are inevitable, the termination policies are fair. This type of management creates a stable environment in which employees are not afraid of a consultant, although they will still be curious and perhaps a little concerned about what the person is doing. On the other hand, in companies where the employees view the personnel policies as harsh or capricious, they are easily alarmed and tend to look on the consultant as a threat.

In companies where the employees dislike management or certain management policies, and realize that the company needs to make changes, they may welcome a consultant, believing that improvements may result. Sometimes they are right. However, if the problem is that the top managers are weak, consultants will not be able to change their personalities or their ways of managing. The consultant cannot shore up a weak executive for very long, although he or she can provide training in good management methods. A weak executive's difficulty is usually in being afraid to make decisions, or making poor decisions based on insufficient information. This the consultant cannot change.

Company Situation

When a company is known to have its back to the wall, its employees may be glad to see a consultant; they feel that the consultant cannot make the situation worse and may possibly improve it.

Mergers and acquisitions, so common in recent years, create great employee uncertainty, particularly for the employees of the company being acquired. The announcement of a merger or acquisition is usually accompanied by a statement from the controlling company, Company A. "The employees of Company B [company being taken over] are our greatest asset," the statement may proclaim. "We plan no changes either in management or in other positions." Most of those involved believe that; nevertheless, the managers of Company A have already begun to plan how they can take over all or part of the authority of their counterparts at Company B.

If consultants are involved in the consolidation process, they usually try to find solutions that are fair to all concerned. However, lower-level employees may not realize this, and tend to blame the consultants for any new arrangements they dislike.

For instance, we were once engaged to make recommendations for a reorganization following upon the acquisition of Company X by Company Y. Both companies were in the same business. They competed in one geographic area. Company X had a better product and a better reputation than Company Y. We recommended that in the area they shared, the combined companies be set up as a separate division, with the management of Company X in charge, and that the best features of X's product be retained. Our recommendations were adopted, but soon thereafter the former manager of X accepted a position with another company, whereupon Y's executives took over the division. Some time later, I found myself in the office of a former employee of X who didn't know me as a consultant. I asked what she thought of the new relationship with Y. She replied, "I hate it. We had a fine company until the so-and-so consultants came in."

Type of Study

This is an age of change. The use of computer technology to plan and control the performance of company activities, the introduction of robots to replace people, are becoming common practices in U.S. industry. While these changes are usually designed to increase efficiency and make U.S. products more competitive at home and abroad, they are unsettling to management, and even more so to the blue-collar employee. Consultants are frequently associated with the introduction of such methods, which, of course, usually result in the elimination of jobs, both at upper and lower levels.

Employees naturally fear any study of a type that is expected to result in the loss of jobs. While these studies can take many forms and are not generally described simply as cost-reduction studies, employees are quick to learn their purpose, however they may be titled.

Of course, consultants undertake many studies in which cost-reduction is not the primary aim. Some appear threatening to the employees, others do not.

Organization studies are perhaps next to cost-reduction studies in creating apprehension, particularly among management-level employees. These studies often involve changes in the management structure, changes in assignments, the combining of positions, changes in goals or objectives, and the like. Employees are uncertain as to how their duties and assignments may be altered, or worse, as to whether their jobs will continue to exist.

Marketing studies are usually considered to be harmless. Studies designed to produce improvements in employee performance by training, job rotation, and the like may actually be greeted with enthusiasm. Management compensation studies, also, are usually well received. However, such studies may produce a general expectation of a salary increase unless suitably explained. They may be described as designed to eliminate inequities, provide financial incentives for better performance, or set up suitable benefit plans.

Smoothing the Path

No matter how careful management may be, the appearance of consultants will probably always cause some employee disquiet, particularly if the consultants' recommendations are likely to involve staff reductions. Nevertheless, there are several steps that can be taken to keep the employee-consultant relationship cooperative rather than adversarial. These steps include: taking appropriate preliminary actions; announcing the study in a reassuring way; securing the consultant's assistance in relieving fear; maintaining a positive attitude during the course of the study.

Preliminary Actions

Before the consultant is brought in, you, the client executive, will presumably have discussed the problem to be addressed with your fellow executives, so that they have either shared in your decision to retain a consultant or, at the least, are prepared for it. While you are in the process of selecting the consultant, you can also decide whom to appoint to act as study coordinator or as members of the study team, if you decide to use either or both. The criteria for their selection are discussed in the next chapter, "Managing the Consulting Assignment."

Just before the consultant arrives, the coordinator, the study team, and appropriate members of management should be informally notified of the consultant's engagement, the nature of the assignment, and why you believe it is necessary. It is well to stress to these executives that they can play a very important role in the study. You will also want to point out that, while undoubtedly many of the ideas for improvement will come from them rather than the consultant, a fresh and knowledgeable point of view combined with their own thinking should produce a better result faster.

Preparing a Suitable
Formal Announcement

Above all, you, as the executive in charge, will want to avoid uninformed employee speculation about the consulting assignment. Where at all possible, it is important that employees be told the true nature of the study. Unexplained studies cause conjecture and fear. If the employees know that consultants are at work on a project of unknown purpose, the situation may cause them to worry from the time they learn about it until the consultant is gone, and afterward. This worry can affect their performances and attitudes.

Hence, appropriate employees should be informed by means of a formal announcement that the company is bringing in a consulting firm, and be provided with a credible explanation of what the consultants will be doing. "Appropriate" employees are all those in the departments where the consultants will be working and any others from whom opinions or information will be sought. This announcement, which should be carefully worded, is best made at the outset of the study. The consultant can help with the wording, but it should be approved by and go out over the signature of the managing executive. The best results are obtained from announcements that emphasize these points:

The Purpose of the Study and Its Importance to the Company. The announcement should explain why the study is needed and what the solution of the problem involved will mean to the company's present and future performance. Emphasis should be placed on the needs for improvement.

The Need for Employee Cooperation. The announcement should also state that management is expecting the employees to make a valuable contribution to the study, and request them to give frank and honest answers to questions relating to the problem that are raised by the consultant. It should also point out that the best results will be achieved by a joint employee-consultant partnership, since the employees have firsthand information on the conditions relating to the problem and can prevent the consultants from arriving at a solution that is interesting but un-workable.

The Nonthreatening Nature of the Study. The announcement should emphasize that the purpose of the study is to appraise functions and activities to see if there are opportunities for improvement, but not to appraise the performance of employees—unless, of course, the purpose of the study is in fact performance evaluation. In that case, it should be stressed that the goal is to determine employee needs for training or experience so as to improve their capabilities either in their present positions or for promotion or both.

The Benefits of Working with Consultants. The announcement should point out the advantages for the employees in an employee-consultant collaboration. It should describe the consultant's qualifications and background, and the types of situation in which the consultant has worked. If possible, it should also provide the names of other companies served by the consultant. If the consultant is not willing to publicize the names of clients, a list of industries with which the person has been involved can be furnished. The educational value of working with consultants should be emphasized: consultants can acquaint employees with new ideas, advanced methods and techniques, and the results of their successful studies at other companies.

The foregoing suggestions are suitable for studies to be carried out in companies in reasonably good financial and organizational health. When the company's existence is threatened, a rather different approach may be required. If employee sacrifices will be essential to keeping the company alive, the employees must be told enough about the seriousness of the company's condition to convince them of the necessity for these sacrifices.

The postderegulation experiences of the large, established carriers in the airline industry underscore this point. These carriers had been operating for years with government-controlled rates and fares and with union contracts that provided for high wage rates and stringent work rules restricting assignments to specific tasks. After deregulation, they found themselves competing with newcomers whose wage rates were less than 50 percent of their own and who were unhampered by restrictive work rules. To get a share of the market, the new carriers reduced their fares to rates as low as half of what the majors were charging. (A few even made a profit.)

The chief executives of the established carriers recognized that, to stay in business, they would need to persuade their employees that their wage rates and work rules must be changed to be competitive with those of the newcomers. After having secured middle management's understanding and cooperation, several chief executives initiated programs of frank announcements, meetings with employees, and news releases describing the companies' dilemma. At least one carrier retained a psychological consultant to help convey the message to its employees. Management set an example by reducing their own salaries first.

In several of these companies the employees, understanding the situation, have now agreed to wage reductions and less restrictive work rules.

In situations where it is not possible to promise employee security, the employees should be told what the company's policies will be should a layoff become necessary. Some companies provide bonuses for early retirement. Some offer severance pay. Some rely on attrition. Sometimes the company provides the services of an outplacement consultant to assist employees who have been laid off to prepare themselves for new positions. Whatever the policies may be, the employees will feel more comfortable if they know what to expect.

There is some question as to whether management should announce studies that do not require the presence of the consultant on the premises and where there is no interviewing of personnel. Ordinarily, when studies are "off-campus," there is no need for an explanation. Often the studies are of such a nature that the results will have no immediate effect on employees; for example, when a privately owned company is planning to go public. Where its impact is likely to be felt soon, it may be better to inform them of the study and its purpose.

Confidential studies pose another special problem. By their very nature, they cannot be described accurately to employees. Sometimes companies mask their purpose by announcing them as information studies, or under some other innocuous title that will alleviate apprehension without being actually dishonest.

Whatever the situation may be, it is always important that the announcement be carefully thought through and properly presented. My personal experiences with two very different management approaches will illustrate the point.

The first example epitomizes the wrong way to introduce a study. This study was initiated by the chairman of the board of a machine tool company. The chairman, who was not an active executive but was the company's major stockholder, had become concerned over the low earnings of the company and their impact on stock performance. He had repeatedly discussed the poor earnings with his CEO, the company president, and the president had merely promised that things would get better in the future and cautioned him not to get impatient. The chairman, at his wit's end, consulted his general counsel, who suggested that he engage a consulting firm. The chairman did not really know what consultants did, but he took the advice of his counsel and asked us to meet with him. He requested us to undertake a performance improvement study, to which we agreed. We offered to help him prepare an announcement, but he did not believe our assistance was needed. The announcement that he sent to the president and his officers was merely a short statement that "we are bringing in the Golightly firm to see if they can be of some assistance to us."

When we arrived, the president and the other members of management were icily polite but completely unforthcoming. They supplied perfunctory answers to our questions but did not provide any information that we did not directly seek. It was obvious that they were frightened but hoped that "this too would pass," since the chairman had never before shown any interest in day-to-day management. We had a great deal of difficulty getting performance information in any depth. However, the causes of the problem were sufficiently obvious so that we did not have to probe very deeply to discover them.

We found that the company was budgeting for sales targets that were never met. Therefore, sales were always overestimated and operating costs were higher than need be, so that profits were low or nonexistent. Also, the company had a costly distribution system which resulted in excessive inventory levels. In addition, two of its divisions were losers, with little or no opportunity to grow or become more profitable.

Our findings and recommendations were politely received by management and promptly filed away. No action was forthcoming. Several months later the general counsel requested that we give him a copy of the report, which we did. He thereupon discussed it with the chairman, who asked that we come back and help the company to implement the report.

The chairman had by now become completely dissatisfied with the president's performance and had made arrangements to bring in a replacement from outside. I have always believed that this could have been avoided if a properly considered announcement had been made at the outset of the study, so that we would have been able to work in a cooperative way with the president and his staff.

The second example is an illustration of an announcement that was carefully prepared. Our client in this case was the president of a large service company. He believed that, while the company was a leader in its industry at present, it needed to take action to maintain that position. He engaged our firm to study what the company was doing, how they were organized to do it, what competitors were doing, and what changes we believed should be made in organization, marketing, or management methods. When we were ready to begin, he issued an announcement, with which we assisted, that read something like this:

"We are bringing in the firm of Golightly &

Co. to work with us to improve our marketing, our product, and our costs. While we know that we are now among the top companies in our industry, if not the leader, we must act to stay ahead. Your ideas and those of our consultants should provide the leadership methods and organization that we need. We do not anticipate radical shifts but believe it is necessary to make orderly changes as conditions require.

"To work with the consultants, we are appointing a study team composed of three members: Mr. X of the Finance Department, Mr. Y of the Marketing Department, and Mr. Z from Human Resources.

"The consulting firm has served numerous companies in related industries, who have recommended them and their services to us. We believe that you will enjoy and benefit from the relationship and look forward to your joint recommendations for the improvement of our company. Your cooperation is requested."

From the outset we received the utmost in cooperation. The comments and suggestions offered by the executives were frank and constructive. We were given any information that we required for the development of our recommendations. We worked freely and easily with

the study team, who treated our findings confi-
dentially. All in all, it was a most successful and
enjoyable engagement, in large part due to the
thoughtful introduction of the study to the employees and to the continued cooperation and
support we received from the study team and the
client.

The Consultant
Can Help to Allay Fear

Once the study is actually under way, the degree
of employee acceptance will depend to a considerable extent on the consultant's behavior. One
of the criteria in selecting this person was whether
you believed that he or she would be able to get
along well with the employees and operate with
a minimum of disruption. Now is the time for
the consultant to exercise these talents for you.

There are certain guidelines that a consultant
should follow in dealing with the company employees. First of all, the person should be truly
professional and stay with the subject under study.
Strict attention to the matter at hand will prevent
the employees from getting the impression that
the consultant is trying to analyze every situation
in the company.

Early in my career I was told by a very wise senior consultant, "Leave some things under the rocks." There will be many opportunities for the consultant to digress and go into other areas, but, unless the matter has been discussed with you and you have agreed to a change in the assignment, the consultant should usually refrain, even though the byways seem a tempting source of further studies.

When conducting interviews with the employees, the consultant should be discreet and not listen to gossip or participate in discussions of employee performance. If the consultant comments on the quality of performance of another employee, the employee being interviewed will become suspicious, realizing that his or her own performance may be similarly evaluated.

The consultant's attitude toward the employees should be helpful and constructive, not critical. If it appears that the consultant is critical, the employees' fears will be intensified.

The consultant's manner should be friendly. The individual should not be standoffish or appear to have come from on high. Employees like a down-to-earth sort of person to whom they can relate.

The consultant should have good work habits,

and should try to conform to the hours of company staff. If the consultant conforms to the company schedule and works hard, employees will be aware of this and will react favorably. They will believe that this person is making an all-out effort to do a good job. If the consultant leaves early every day and does not seem to be engrossed in the assignment, employees will be critical.

Most consultants know that they should follow these rules, but like other people they sometimes fall short of perfection. It does no harm for you to remind the consultant that it will be very helpful to the company if he or she gets along well with the employees, observes their work schedules, and does not participate in any personal gossip or matters outside the scope of the study. You can point out that the employees are somewhat concerned about a consultant being brought in and that anything he can do to allay their fears will be greatly appreciated.

A *Positive Attitude*
on the Part of the Client

An important factor in calming employee apprehensions during the course of the study is the behavior of the executive in charge. If you, the client, maintain a positive attitude toward the study and the consultant, it will do much to make the employees confident that the study is on track and will produce good results for the company. Although you will naturally be interested in the employees' opinion of the consultant and the approach, it is best that this interest not be too obvious. If the employees feel that you are probing for their reactions, they will believe that you do not have confidence in the consultant, and this will increase their uneasiness.

You will, of course, want to keep up with the consultant's progress. This is best done through the consultant's interim reports, but you will almost certainly receive unsolicited employee comments about the consultant and his or her activities. It is advisable to discourage negative comments, unless the situation appears to be serious. In that event, you will want to conduct an investigation of the consultant's performance, particularly the methods used in working with employees and whether the individual is staying on track. If this investigation discloses major deficiencies, the consultant should be dismissed.

Such situations occur very seldom. Ordinarily, the consultant will be pursuing the study according to the agreement and will be making every effort to secure employee acceptance. Your positive support will help to obtain and keep employee confidence.

To sum up, while you may not be able to eliminate completely employee uneasiness caused by bringing in a consultant to assist in solving a problem, by taking the recommended actions you can reduce it and get general support in working toward a satisfactory solution.

CHAPTER

7

MANAGING
THE
CONSULTING
ASSIGNMENT

Fairly often in my consulting experience, I have encountered an executive who felt that, once a consultant had been selected and told what the problem was, the client had done enough and could go on to other matters. Unfortunately, it isn't quite that simple.

If selecting the consultant wisely is half the battle, there is no doubt that managing the assignment well is the other half. No matter how capable, a consultant can easily go astray if proper direction and support is not received from the client. An executive who sets up a mechanism for keeping control over the assignment and providing leadership to the consultant is likely to get much better results than one who does not.

Not surprisingly, most consultants respond favorably to signs of interest and friendliness. They will work harder and more intelligently when they know that they are not operating in a vacuum. If the assignment is conducted properly, you, the client, and the consultant should arrive at a partnership in which both can express themselves freely, to their mutual benefit. Bear in mind at all times that the goal is to arrive at recommendations and to achieve actions from which you can get full value.

The suggestions that follow are tailored for the most common type of consulting assignment, which involves a period of fact-finding, subsequent development of recommendations, and finally the presentation of findings, recommendations, and an action plan. Of course, the approach is slightly different when the consultant comes in only to perform a specific task, such as conducting a seminar. Common sense will dictate the necessary modifications.

The Study Coordinator

There are a few steps that should be taken before the consultant arrives on the scene. We have already discussed the preparation of the employees and touched on the designation of an executive to act as study coordinator. This person will serve as the point of contact for the consultant. It will be the coordinator's function to set up appointments, provide the consultant with reports and data as needed, and generally keep tabs on the consultant's actions within the company. If an employee has a complaint about the consultant, or vice versa, it will first go to the employee's supervisor and eventually to the coordinator. The coordinator will see that appointments are kept and that reports are given by the consultant to management on the date specified, and in general act as company administrator for the assignment.

Whom to appoint as coordinator depends on the circumstances. When the company or division involved is small, the executive in charge may wish to act as administrator. If not, the executive should appoint another executive who is fair-minded, knows company operations, and commands respect within the company.

There are certain advantages to you, the client executive, in appointing someone else to be coordinator. It permits you to maintain a friendly relationship with the consultant without getting bogged down in administrative details or taking excessive time from your regular duties. It also puts you in a position to act as arbitrator if any disputes arise.

The Study Team

As previously mentioned, it is often helpful both
to the consultant and to management to have a
study team of company employees work along
with the consultant in fact-finding and developing recommendations. The study team should
understand how the company operates and should
be able to save the consultant considerable time.
Besides giving employees confidence that all sides
of the question are being looked at, the team will
gain a thorough understanding of the problem
situation and the consultant's thinking that will
be helpful when the time comes to implement
the ultimate recommendations.

A side benefit is that the experience should be
educational for the study team. Our firm once
did a study involving the organizational relationships of a major corporation—the elimination of
levels of management, the concentration of authority for developing policy to corporate headquarters, the delegation of line authority for
carrying out policies to local levels, and so on. A
team consisting of one up-and-coming executive
from each of the departments concerned worked
with us in developing our findings and recommendations and presenting our report. Not only

did these executives help us materially in getting our report accepted and implemented, but also all but one of them went on to become a company president or division head. I like to believe that the insights they gained in the course of our study had something to do with their rise.

Of course, if the consultant will be working in a particularly sensitive area, a study team from the company may be inappropriate.

If you do plan to use a study team, the members should be selected before the consultant's arrival. Bright young staff people are particularly suitable candidates for this type of work.

Office Space and Clerical Support

You will want to provide the consultant with suitable office space to encourage working on company premises. You will also want to provide adequate support services, especially if the consultant charges separately for report preparation and clerical expenses, as is customary. Consultants charges are usually considerably higher than your company's in-house costs. Of course, if the material is of a confidential nature, it is better that the report be prepared by the consultant's staff and in the consultant's offices rather than yours.

Getting the Study Under Way

When the preparations are completed and the time comes for the consultant to begin work, it is worthwhile to take a little trouble to be sure that the individual gets off to a good start. Naturally, I am not suggesting that you greet the consultant with brass bands or girls throwing flowers, but you do want to give his or her arrival sufficient importance so that both the consultant and the company employees who may be involved realize that you take a personal interest in the success of the project.

Welcome the consultant or consultants—junior consultants are often involved at this stage—review the assignment with them, make sure there is a common understanding, and try to make them feel at home on the premises. If you will not be coordinating the study yourself, introduce the study coordinator and explain what the coordinator will be doing. Emphasize that you will always be ready to visit with the consultants yourself when they feel that they need to talk with you.

If you plan to use a study team, introduce them and explain to the consultants how you expect them to work with the team. Make it clear that the study is the consultants' responsibility and that the team, working under the direction of the consultants, is to assist in any way that will be productive. It is important to stress the confidentiality of their findings to the study team in the presence of the consultant, who will be solely responsible for making reports to management.

Show the consultants where they will be working and let them know that they are welcome to spend as much time as possible on the premises. You want the consultants to get to know the company, its employees, and the working conditions.

Establishing Control

The agreement or contract with the consultant is, of course, the primary control tool. However, there are several matters that such agreements usually do not cover. You will want to reach an understanding about these at the outset.

Out-of-Pocket Expenses. To the extent feasible, the consultants should follow company policy on travel, lodging, and meals. For instance, if company executives travel first class and lower-level employees travel coach, the status of the consultant should determine the class to be used. (The managing consultant will probably travel first class and the others coach.) The same standards should apply to hotels and meals.

Clerical and Other Support Services. As previously pointed out, clerical services can usually be provided more inexpensively by the client than by the consultant. If it is appropriate, you will want to let the consultant know that you expect to provide these services.

Work Habits. Let the consultants know that you hope they will keep the same work hours as company office staff. Explain that, while you realize they cannot always keep to a strict schedule, unusual work hours will subject them to employee criticism.

Company Meetings. When there are to be a number of consultants working on the assignment and their work will involve attending company meetings, it is well to check up on how many meetings they plan to attend and how many will be at each meeting. Sometimes more consultants want to attend meetings than is necessary.

The Study Plan

Most consultants write out a study plan for themselves at the beginning of the assignment. This plan can also be a very useful control tool for the client; it is a good idea to ask the consultant to give you a copy. The plan usually includes:

The objectives of the study as defined in the agreement with the client.

The information needed and where and how it is planned to secure it. This information may come from statistical data, company reports, and/or interviews with employees. It depends somewhat on the nature of the study, but the consultant will usually want to interview selected employees who have a personal knowledge of the area being studied that may not be included in the statistical data.

A schedule of work: the amount of time to be spent in securing data; the time to be spent in reviewing it and developing recommendations; and the dates for delivering a report or reports to the client.

Who is to secure the information needed and who is to conduct each interview. There may be certain interviews where members of the study team, if there is one, should not be present. Usually only one or two interviewers are needed at each session. Individual interviews with each client executive will produce the best results.

If the consultant has not prepared a study plan, ask for a timetable for the various stages of the study.

The study plan should provide for frequent interim reports to keep the client informed of the consultant's activities. If the study plan does not provide for interim reports, you should request them. Ask also for the dates on which they will be delivered and the subjects to be discussed.

Providing Leadership

In addition to welcoming the consultants when they arrive, you should plan to hold frequent informal meetings with them just to see how they are getting along, whether they have any problems, and so on. These meetings should be apart from the coordinating function, even if you act as your own administrator. You want the consultants to feel that you are personally interested in the study and that it is important to the company.

You will want to keep the consultants informed of any changes in company operations, policy, or performance that might affect their work.

Employee Participation

Employees should be encouraged to cooperate with the consultant to the extent possible, both in making themselves available and in supplying information.

Of course, employees have their regular duties to perform, but every effort should be made to arrange their schedules so that they can give the consultant the time required. Appointments should be scheduled in advance; if the employee cannot keep an appointment the consultant should be notified soon enough to permit scheduling of his or her time elsewhere.

"Be frank and open with the consultant," is

usually the company watchword. Naturally, the consultant is expected to confine requests for information to matters pertinent to the study. Where there is any doubt as to the appropriateness of the consultant's questions, the matter should be referred to the employee's supervisor or the study coordinator.

Keeping in Touch:
the Interim Report

It goes without saying that you will want to keep track of the progress of the study. The coordinator, and your own observation, will tell you what the consultant is doing; the interim reports should tell you the direction in which the consultant is heading.

The senior consultant should submit these reports to you frequently. Interim reports are usually given at intervals of about a month, depending somewhat on the nature and duration of the assignment. The interim report, which is usually oral rather than written, should keep you informed of progress, findings-to-date, and tentative conclusions.

You will want to allow time for discussion after the report is delivered. If you have any doubts about the direction the consultant's work is taking, or about the consultant's activities in general, this will be a good opportunity to discuss it. If the consultant is having any difficulties, he or she will have a chance to air them.

The principal reasons for providing interim reports have already been given. However, these reports can serve another purpose—educating the client. In a situation several years ago, we were brought into a company to develop a type of organization that would permit the CEO to delegate authority and prepare for a successor. One phase of the recommendation involved setting up product managers. It was necessary to provide performance information about each product line for the product managers. Previously, the company had provided information on a divisional basis only and really had very little information about performance results from each product line.

The chief executive authorized the development of the product information system but did not understand why it was needed, since he did not as yet have full understanding of the product managers' role. The information study was a lengthy one, and no interim reports were required or given. At the end of the study, the chief executive accepted the report and authorized its implementation, but never used the new information to evaluate product managers' results. He still used only the divisional information and did not properly hold product managers responsible for the performance of their respective product lines. In retrospect, I realize that, had we given him interim reports and stressed the purpose of this system, we could probably have convinced him of its usefulness. The supervision and management of product managers was inadequate until several years later when a new president came in and the reports were properly used.

It often happens that, as a consultant's work progresses, problems are discovered that are not within the scope of the study as originally understood, but which the consultant thinks bear importantly on the matters under review. If this occurs, the consultant will presumably let you know about it when the interim report is made, and you can decide together whether the original limits of the assignment should be changed.

While you will, of course, want to discourage any desire the consultant may show to spend the next ten years investigating your company from top to bottom, you should guard against dismissing any insights too lightly. Consultants, who are not involved in the chain of command and who have had experience with many different organizations, are often able to put their fingers on trouble spots management has not noticed or to map the forest where management has only seen the trees.

For instance, our firm was once called in by a major entrepreneur to do a study of his administrative organization. Although he had vast holdings, he was having difficulty in meeting his financial obligations and thought that he might be spending too much on staff. We quickly discovered that his organizational expenses were tiny in relation to his total financial commitments and began an evaluation of his cash requirements, cash flow, and assets to see what he might sell to settle his debts, or failing that, to develop an overall plan to convince his principal creditors to extend long-term credit.

When he realized what we were doing, the entrepreneur, an imperious person, pointed out that we had been retained to do an organization study and only an organization study. He ordered us to desist from delving into his affairs further. We, of course, complied. As far as the original understanding was concerned, he was perfectly correct, but it is also true that he was forced into bankruptcy a few months later.

If the scope of the assignment does change, you will want to work out a supplemental written agreement along the lines discussed in earlier chapters.

It is well to require the consultant to give you tentative conclusions as each interim report is made. Not only will this force the consultant to organize and analyze findings as work progresses, it will also give you an idea of what the final recommendations are likely to be and what actions you will need to take to implement them.

Do not be disturbed when the consultant stops the fact-finding process and withdraws to begin his analysis of the significance of the information gathered to prepare a report containing the findings and recommendations. This phase of the study usually requires at least as much time as the fact-finding.

If you have chosen the consultant wisely and kept in touch as work has progressed, it is very unlikely that you will find yourself totally dissatisfied with the consultant's activities or the direction his or her thinking is taking. However, if you do find that you cannot reach agreement on the proper line of attack, or if you conclude for some other reason that the consultant cannot produce the results you expected, you will want to arrange to terminate the study with a minimum of upheaval. The circumstances and the terms of your agreement will determine whether you act at once or wait until the assignment has been completed and a report has been delivered.

Getting Appropriate Results: The Recommendations

If you are familiar with the way consultants work, you will know that, when the consultant has completed the study, the findings and recommendations will normally be submitted in the form of a written report. The consultant will expect to present a summary of its contents in a meeting with you and any other executives you may select, possibly employing charts, graphs, or other visual material. This presentation is a crucial part of the consulting assignment. It will provide a basis for future corrective action. When scheduling it, you will want to allow ample uninterrupted time not only to hear what the consultant has to say, but also to permit answers to any questions you or your colleagues may have.

Try to keep the atmosphere at the presentation meeting friendly and pleasant. It is very possible that the consultant will be unable to address your problems without saying something unflattering about your company's performance, and perhaps even your own. This may not be agreeable to you, no matter how tactful the consultant may be. It is best to prepare yourself to think of the comments as constructive, which, of course, they should be.

I have worried a good deal in my time over how to tell clients things I thought they might not want to hear. I particularly remember one client situation in which it was obvious that the president and CEO, who was brilliant at forward planning and policy development, was not a good day-to-day manager or communicator. After gathering all the evidence, we concluded that we should recommend he hire an executive vice president and general manager to take over day-to-day administration of the company.

The president was a prestigious and aloof man who did not invite conversation. When time came to present our report, I worried for days how he would receive what might seem like a denigration of his abilities. If I had not psyched myself up for the presentation, I would have been tempted to fall in with an associate's suggestion that we put off telling him to another day.

As it happened, the president accepted the

recommendations readily, with no sign of annoyance, and immediately began an in-house search for a suitable candidate. He selected a very capable and well-liked executive. The company's performance soon improved. That is the kind of response every consultant hopes for.

Provided that the consultant is competent and that you have been overseeing the progress and giving your viewpoint through discussion of the interim reports, the recommendations produced should meet your needs. In large companies where higher and lower echelon executives will be involved in implementation, you will, of course, need to secure their understanding and/or cooperation. You will find this helpful if not essential even in a smaller company.

When the actions recommended cannot be carried out without the approval of higher level executives or the board of directors, it is frequently helpful to have the consultant make the presentation again for their benefit. At the least, the consultant will reinforce your own request for action. If persuasive and well known in the field, or associated with a prestigious consulting firm, the consultant may be able to secure their agreement where you could not.

It is also valuable to have the consultant make

the presentation to the middle-level executives who will be charged with implementing the recommendations. They are likely to be cautious about expressing themselves and reluctant to see the status quo changed, so in assessing their reactions you will need to do a certain amount of reading between the lines. Nevertheless, they can often make important contributions. In any case, having the consultant make the presentation will help to ensure that they understand the plan and will work wholeheartedly to put it into effect. Many good plans have been spoiled by executives who implemented them improperly.

Once they have heard the recommendations, the other executives concerned (usually your subordinates or peers) will be in a position to give you their views about their viability and the cost of implementing them, as well as to what actions should be taken first. Even the most capable, conscientious consultant cannot assess all the possible consequences of his or her recommendations. This is particularly true when the organization concerned is large or when the recommendations involve major changes in the company's methods of operation. You will want to get as much input as is practical from the other executives before going ahead.

If a study team from the company has worked on the consulting assignment, it will be useful to have them attend the presentations. Not only can their insights be valuable, you will want them to feel that they are still on the team, particularly since they can be very helpful when the time for implementation comes. They may be called on to assist in presenting the report.

The Consultant's Role in Implementation

Unless your original agreement specifies otherwise, the consultant's job is finished when the recommendations are presented. However, there are many circumstances in which you may need the consultant's help in putting the plans into practice. Some consultants will not accept an assignment of certain types, unless their assistance in implementation is provided for.

The consultant's assistance is especially desirable when implementing recommendations that involve changes in organization and the ways in which individuals or departments interact to accomplish their tasks, and/or work methods and procedures. It is often useful for the consultant to hold work sessions with the employees concerned to demonstrate how the changes will affect the way they perform their duties and to illustrate with problem-solving examples. Such meetings also provide an opportunity to assess employee reaction to the recommendations and the impact of their implementation. In some cases, on-the-job coaching may be needed, followed by periodic checks to make sure that the plans are being properly carried out. The consultant may use these work sessions to revise recommendations to better suit the situation if need be and still maintain their objectives. The consultant may also be helpful when the recommended changes cut across departmental or divisional lines. The company's chief executive is likely to be too busy to oversee the implementation himself, and lower-level executives may encounter political difficulties.

The consultant understands all of the elements needed to make a new concept effective, whether it be a plan of organization or a new system, and is not biased by personal desires. He or she is often needed to keep the proper balance and to ensure that implemented actions are consistent with the recommendations.

A few years ago our firm encountered a situation that exemplified this problem. We had been asked to study the adequacy of a large company's financial organization and to find a new chief financial officer. We discovered that not only was there a deficiency in the necessary financial skills, but also that various departments were carrying out financial planning and control activities more or less independently. We recommended that the company's financial function be strengthened and centralized under its newly appointed chief financial officer. We also recommended that we be retained to assist him in the implementation process.

The company management accepted our recommendations as to organization and staffing, but not our proposal to help in implementing them. They believed that the chief financial officer could successfully accomplish the task himself.

Three years later the chief financial officer resigned, whereupon the chief executive asked us to search for a replacement and also to investigate the general state of the financial function. We found that the departed executive had put into effect most of the recommended changes that were under his direct control. Changes that involved other departments had not been made, particularly in the budgeting plan buildup and budget compliance. Presumably it had simply been too politically difficult a task for him to secure the necessary cooperation from other executives more or less on his own level. In accepting the assignment to search for a new executive, we required that we assist in implementation of our recommendations.

Whether the consultant is officially retained to assist in the implementation or not, he or she will remain interested in its success. After all, a person's professional reputation depends on the results achieved by clients. Most consultants will make every effort to work with clients on an ad hoc basis if they encounter unexpected difficulties.

When, as sometimes happens, implementation of the recommendations must be totally or partially postponed, the consultant will appreciate being told the reason. No one likes to see work thrown away, even if one has been paid for it. If you should need the consultant in the future, he or she will be much more likely to put forth maximum effort for you if it is known that the recommendations are taken seriously.

To sum up, you can manage the assignment and the consultant to secure the product you desire

and are paying for. It will require your support
to motivate, to secure common understanding of
the objectives of the study, and to bring about
the proper interplay between the consultant and
company personnel for best results.

CHAPTER

8

EVALUATING
THE
PROJECT

There is one sure way of measuring the value of a consultant's work: by the successful results of the implementation of his recommendations. If the problem you engaged him to deal with no longer exists after his departure, there can be very little question that a good job has been done. Conversely, if all the recommendations have been put into effect and your company finds its position unimproved, or even worsened, there is certainly something wrong somewhere.

In many cases, however, it is impossible to make an immediate appraisal on this basis. The recommendations may take some time to implement, or they may be of such a nature that the results will emerge only gradually, or the whole implementation process may have been delayed for one reason or another. In such situations a judgment of the consultant's effectiveness will have to be based on less clear-cut standards.

In spite of the possible difficulties involved, I nevertheless recommend that you, the executive in charge, attempt to evaluate the consultant's work within a month or so of the completion of the study, while all the circumstances are still fresh in your mind. This evaluation will be helpful in several ways.

It will stimulate you to reassess the recommendations to see whether modifications are needed.

It will serve to remind you of the importance of putting the consultant's plan into practice, if this implementation is not already complete.

It will give you an opportunity to review your own dealings with the consultant to see whether there are any steps you could have taken to make the person's work more effective. If so, you will want to make a mental note to apply your insights should you have occasion to engage consultants in the future.

It will assist you in determining whether to use the consultant again.

In listing these benefits, I have assumed that you are at least moderately well pleased with the consultant's recommendations. I hope that no one who has read this book will have engaged a totally unsatisfactory consultant. Even if that should happen, however, I believe you will find it worthwhile to take another look at the study and the conditions under which it was carried out. There may very well be something to be learned from such a reappraisal.

The Product

The first and most important question is, did you get the product you expected? If the study produced the actions that led or will lead to solving the problem with which the consultant was brought in to deal, you may say that you did. If the results are still in any way in doubt, there are a number of other questions that should be asked.

The Recommendations

At the conclusion of the study, you presumably received the consultant's recommendations, supported by findings and conclusions. Were the recommendations on target? Were they logical and properly supported by factual material? Do you believe that they provided a practical solution to the problem or situation?

If not, was it the consultant who was at fault? Did you identify the problem correctly? Did you state the problem and your objectives clearly, so that the consultant could understand? A consultant has no magical powers, and is unlikely to solve a problem that he or she is unaware of. As Young & Rubicam Board Chairman Edward Ney remarked recently when I asked his opinion of the use of consultants, "If the user understands what he is looking for and can articulate same— it works well, like most things."

Did you provide the consultant with proper support and assistance? Was the consultant able to arrange suitable and timely interviews and readily obtain the information required?

If the consultant's solution was unsatisfactory to you, did you really want the problem solved? Sometimes executives are torn between doing things in what they feel is the proper way and following behavior patterns that have been successful for them in the past.

In this connection, I am reminded of a self-made millionaire who was sent to me by a client when I first established my own consulting firm. This man, a typical entrepreneur, was the principal owner of a business that he had built from scratch. His company's sales volume amounted to about $450 million a year, with good products and an excellent record of growth.

I asked the potential client why he felt that he needed a consultant, since he was apparently getting along very well without anyone else's help.

"Our company has never had an organization plan," he said, "and we believe that we must have one if the company is to grow."

"Are you sure you want a plan of organization?" I said. "Before the study is finished, you may come to believe that it will be a noose around your neck, or at least a rein that will curb you in."

"I must have an organization structure if we are to continue to grow, which we will," he said. "I will do my best to work within it."

After considerable further discussion and with some reluctance, we accepted the assignment. At first the client made us most welcome, but as we began to test our findings and recommendations with him, he grew more and more unresponsive. He had been accustomed to being involved in every detail of his operation, from the cleanliness of the facility, to marketing, to arranging financing. Now he was beginning to realize that a formal organization plan would limit his sphere of activity. He would have to delegate authority and responsibility.

We proceeded with the study and eventually submitted our recommendations. He partially accepted them, but could not immediately bring himself to delegate authority. As I had suspected he would, he found it extremely difficult to work within preordained limits. However, he was a persistent man. Two years later he came back and asked us to make some modifications of our original recommendations and to help with implementing them.

Impact of the Recommendations on Other Company Operations

In assessing the value of the consultant's recommendations, it is important to ask whether their potential impact on other parts of the company was considered. Sometimes it is possible to solve one problem and create another. For example, if we recommend that a company increase its sales, this may make it necessary for the manufacturing operation to be provided with new facilities and additional equipment.

I recall an instance in which a company had retained a consultant to help in strengthening its marketing function. The consultant, together with the head of marketing, developed a plan that forecast a growth in sales of about 100 percent for the following year. The consultant, knowing little about production, made no recommendations as to any changes that might be required in the company's manufacturing facilities.

When the company president reviewed the plan, he realized that it would require a considerable expenditure to enable the company to manufacture its product at the level projected. However, he had some doubts about this projected sales level. He therefore refrained from making any substantial increases in the company's manufacturing capacity.

This turned out to be a very wise course of action. No additional capacity was needed, since the sales target was not reached. As a matter of fact, the company barely exceeded its sales volume for the preceding year.

Nevertheless, the consultant was remiss in omitting manufacturing from his calculations.

Had the marketing forecast been correct, the company would have been in a pickle.

Implementation

The way in which the consultant's recommendations are carried out is so crucial to success that, as previously stated, many consulting firms will not accept an assignment unless they are permitted to take part in the implementation process. Over the years I have seen many good plans wrecked because the client was timid or dilatory about putting them into practice.

Hence, if you have accepted the consultant's recommendations, it is important to ask yourself whether you have done everything possible to implement them. If the answer is yes, you can then go on to ask what the results were. Were they what you anticipated or hoped for? Is it too early to judge? Did the consultant participate in the implementation? Should the consultant have participated? Did he or she offer to assist?

If the recommendations originally appeared to be practical but turn out to be unworkable or impossible to implement, it is probably the fault of the consultant. More testing should have been done before the plan was submitted. Sometimes, however, recommendations need only be slightly modified to make them workable. If the consultant is assisting with implementation, he or she may make or suggest the proper changes.

Of course, you yourself can make changes as you proceed. However, you will want to be sure that your alterations do not destroy the concept or purpose of the recommended course of action, as they did in the following situation. We had been asked to develop the organization structure for a newly created position, president and general manager, reporting to the chairman and chief executive officer. We concluded that the president should direct not only marketing and manufacturing but several other activities as well, including product improvement, industrial relations, and budget planning and control. Our purpose was to make the president truly accountable for the company's results.

At the conclusion of the study, we made a formal presentation to the chairman, the president, and the financial vice president. At this presentation, the financial vice president made a strong argument for the direction of budgets to continue to be part of his own responsibility. He maintained that he would provide the newly appointed president with all the information he required on a timely basis. The president finally agreed, over our objections. The chairman, who had previously accepted our original plan, did not interfere.

When the new structure was put in place, the financial vice president failed to give the president time and the proper financial support and information. The president always received performance data late, and this placed him at a great disadvantage. He had insufficient time to take appropriate actions on controlling costs or improving sales. He resigned two years later.

At that point the marketing vice president was promoted to the post of president, with control over the budget. One year later the financial vice president resigned.

While the change requested by the financial vice president appeared reasonable on the surface, actually it destroyed the concept of holding the president fully accountable for results. Once this had been demonstrated, our original plan was put into effect.

The Consultant's Methods

After you have given due consideration to the consultant's product, you will want to assess the person's way of working. Of course, you will not attach the same importance to the consultant's work methods that you do to the product. A consultant who discovers a neat and satisfactory solution for a difficult problem can be forgiven a few lapses; one whose recommendations are worthless is of very little use no matter how diligent and professional the person may seem. Still, the way the consultant goes about the task does influence the way the company employees feel about the individual and about you as the sponsor, and about the recommendations made. It is also a fairly reliable indication of the sort of person the consultant is.

Adherence to Proposal

One of the first questions to be asked is, was the study performed within the time and at the fee originally estimated? If so, the consultant gets a very good mark. If not, were the objectives of the study altered so that more information was required than was originally anticipated? Were appointments difficult to schedule? These or other causes for delay beyond the consultant's control could be responsible for the overruns. Did the consultant notify you when it became clear that

the study would require additional time and fees?
If so, and you agreed, consider the study completed on schedule and give the consultant a good
mark—an A + if the agreement was confirmed
in writing.

If the consultant spent more time than planned
without notifying you, do you believe this extra
time was justified? Are you agreeable to paying
the additional fees involved? If so, the consultant
will be entitled to passing marks.

If it appears that the consultant has been
accumulating additional charges for no good
reason, these charges should not be paid. The
person's performance should be considered unsatisfactory.

Over- and
Under-Researching

What about the amount of time the consultant
spent in researching the project? Was more, or
less, information acquired than was necessary?
An overthorough consultant can waste a great deal
of time. On the other hand, the consultant cannot be expected to give you an answer that will
have real validity with no research. Enough
background on the situation causing the problem

must be obtained to properly determine what actions are needed to correct it. Just how much
information is enough is a matter of judgment.

I have known several cases of both over- and
under-researching. One of the first consulting
studies I took part in concerned communications
between the corporate headquarters of a company and one of its subsidiaries. In the first week
we learned that there were no corporate policies
to guide the performance of the subsidiary, and
no plan or budget through which to delegate authority, so that headquarters was controlling every
decision. During the next several weeks we studied every oral and written communication between the two from the vantage point of both the
sender and the recipient. We learned nothing
new. The vast amount of additional research was
wasted.

On the other hand, a consultant may do insufficient research to grasp the dynamics of a
situation. For instance, I once knew a senior
consultant who believed that the way to develop
an organization plan was to sit down with the
chief executive and obtain a statement of the duties and responsibilities of each key executive.
From this, the consultant developed an organization chart. His rationale: "Who would know

more about company organization than the chief executive?" Unfortunately, his chart had little to do with the way the company really worked. He ignored the opinions and problems of the other company executives and their ideas on what was needed to improve performance. He also failed to identify the factors crucial to the success of the company and to fix responsibility for them appropriately.

To sum up, the consultant may have gathered too much information, the wrong type of information, or too little information. You must judge as best you can.

The Consultant's
Interviewing Techniques

What is your opinion of the way in which the consultant conducted interviews? Was the person able to ask questions of company personnel without seeming to be disapproving? Sometimes a consultant will ask questions in a way that implies adverse criticism. The person being interviewed, of course, reacts unfavorably, and may get the impression that the consultant thinks little of the company, its methods generally, and the employee.

Sometimes the consultant goes too far the other way, and in an attempt to ingratiate himself or herself, will gush with enthusiasm about the company, its executives, its products, and so on. The interviewee soon sees through this technique.

Most people are not fully responsive to either the critical or the overly friendly method of interviewing. Best results are obtained by the consultant who asks straightforward, pertinent questions in a relaxed, pleasant manner.

The Consultant's Relations with the Employees (and You)

Respect For the Consultant. Employees don't have to like the consultant, but they should respect him or her. Did the consultant earn this respect? Did the employees feel that the person was knowledgeable about the matter being studied? Did they believe that the consultant behaved in a proper and professional way?

Able consultants sometimes do foolish things that cause them to lose the respect of the employees and the client. I once knew a very able consultant, for example, who started dating one of the client company secretaries and confided his opinion of the company and some of its employees to her. Of course, these opinions quickly became known throughout the company, and his usefulness was at an end. Another consultant, whose client was the company's head of marketing, got the impression that his client had a low opinion of the company's chief executive. The consultant was unwise enough to tell the client that he considered the chief executive inept. The client used his remarks with the chief executive to get himself promoted and the consultant fired.

Work Habits. Did the consultant's work habits conform to those of the company? Were appointments kept? Did you get the impression that the consultant was a hard worker, or seemed to be dillydallying on the job? Were the necessary interim reports provided, so that you were kept informed of progress and of preliminary findings? If not, the consultant's relationship with you was not proper.

Some consultants who are clever at diagnosing a situation fail to do the necessary spadework. I remember a certain consultant, "old Hank," who was one of the most brilliant diagnosticians I have ever known. He could analyze a problem and lay out a study plan to secure a solution in a very capable and professional way. Beyond that he was useless. Put him in charge of a study, and he sat in his office reading almost anything but information relating to the study. He seldom ventured outside to find out what the other consultants were learning until the time came for report development and presentation. He would then fill himself in enough to take a leading role in presentation, although not in preparing the report. His sins finally caught up with him when questions from a client revealed that his knowledge was superficial and that he was unfamiliar with details or supporting information.

Client employees are quick to separate the drones from the workers. If you are in doubt about the consultant's diligence, the people with whom he or she worked should be able to enlighten you.

Honesty vs. Tact. It is important that the consultant be frank and honest in presenting findings. This may be difficult, because during the course of the study the consultant has probably become friendly with you and other employees and hesitates to say things that may cause harm to relationships or damage any chances of securing future studies. Nevertheless, a certain degree of candor is essential in analyzing most problems.

If you feel that the consultant was abrasive, it may be wise to ask yourself whether what you saw as harshness may simply have been a straightforward evaluation of the situation and its causes.

It is up to you to decide whether the consultant struck the proper balance between performing the study with a minimum of disruption and providing you with an honest report that met the needs of the situation.

This whole evaluation process sounds more time-consuming than in fact it really is. You will find that you can answer most of the questions very quickly, and I believe you will discover that the time you spend has been put to good use. Not only will the evaluation help you to make the maximum use of the study just completed, it will also provide guidelines for selecting and making the best use of consultants in the future.

CHAPTER

9

SEVEN OPPORTUNITIES MISSED BY CLIENTS

Most of the managements I have known over the years have been conscientious, able, and prompt to solve problems and to seize any opportunities for improvement. Occasionally, however, I have encountered situations in which managements failed to act wisely, in which they overlooked chances to increase profits and growth, in spite of, or sometimes even because of, warnings from a consultant.

What were the reasons for these executive failures? Although they varied widely, many of them were traceable to the kind of judgmental errors discussed in the following pages. The examples I have chosen are, I believe, typical of the situations in which management is less than fully effective. I hope that these histories will influence the thinking of readers who may at some point face similar challenges.

Failure to Recognize
Competitor's Capabilities

The story of Company X and its chief executive illustrates how important it is for management to consider external as well as internal conditions.

Company X produced and marketed an extensive line of toiletries. The company was showing a reasonable yearly profit, but no real growth. One of its products, "Salask," was responsible for 40 percent of its sales volume and 50 percent of its profits. Its other products were achieving only mediocre sales and profits. The company devoted little effort or funds to research and development, and had not introduced a new product in years.

Company X's principal competitor, Company Y, carried on extensive research activities. It had an enviable record of successfully introducing new or improved products. All of its products received heavy promotional and advertising support.

Company X's chief executive believed that the best way to improve his firm's performance would be to improve the way in which its products were marketed. He accordingly called in our firm to develop a new, product-focused marketing organization.

We proceeded with the marketing reorganization study according to the terms of our agreement. In the course of this study, we became aware of the company's heavy dependence on Salask and of the formidable competition its other product lines encountered from those of Company Y. When we presented our findings, we recommended that in addition to changing its marketing organization, the company increase its expenditures for market research, product improvement, and promotion so as to be competitive with Company Y, and that it acquire new product lines so that it would not need to rely so heavily on Salask.

Company X's chief executive accepted and installed our marketing organization plan. We were not, however, able to convince him of the importance of our other recommendations.

A year later Company Y introduced a new product that was competitive with Salask and had superior qualities. This new product received strong promotional and advertising support. Salask's sales fell rapidly. The profits of Company X were seriously eroded.

Company X's board of directors became seriously concerned. They replaced the CEO with a younger, more dynamic company executive. This executive implemented all of our recommendations. Sales and profits improved, but growth was slow, and it was several years before the company regained a comfortable profit level.

Distrust of the Consultant

It is not unusual for a consultant working on one problem to come across another which the consultant is better equipped to solve than are the company's executives. The announcement of this discovery, however, may be met with suspicion. The client executives may believe that the consultant's real concern is to develop other assignments. It is true that such a motivation is not unknown. Nevertheless, the client would be wise to consider the merits of the consultant's recommendation carefully, lest a real opportunity be lost.

Here, for instance, is a typical example from my own experience.

We had performed a survey of the Yabo Company, a privately owned, successful producer and marketer of capital goods that had recently been acquired by a conglomerate, our client. Yabo had a stable of capable marketing and management talent, fiercely loyal to the company. Its products were highly regarded in the marketplace, and the company was reasonably profitable.

It seemed to us that, successful though the company was, considerable opportunities existed for increasing profits by improving its cost control techniques. We accordingly recommended that we be retained to develop and help to establish such a system.

Our client also felt improvements in profits were needed at Yabo, and that the logical solution was to replace its chief executive. We strongly disagreed, but our motives were suspect; carrying out our recommendations would have involved further work by our firm. The client went ahead with the replacement plan, bringing in a new CEO from outside the company.

The discharge of the original president and the introduction of this new executive had a disastrous effect on company morale. Many of the other executives resigned; some of the rest were fired. Most, if not all, of those that left went on to better jobs elsewhere. Yabo's sales and profits plunged. The next year, after a heavy loss, the new president was replaced in his turn by a former Yabo executive. However, the move came too late. Unnecessary damage had been done that was impossible to repair. Yabo has never regained its former position.

Inability to Make Decisions

The quest for the perfect, totally acceptable solution to any given problem can waste so much time that a whole new set of problems spring up while the search goes on. Consider the following case.

Our firm was asked to develop a strategic plan for a company that had just acquired a president who disliked making decisions. He kept the company's other executives in conference most of the time, always trying to reach a consensus. Literally all the top management executives were involved in committee meetings the first two days of every week, and frequently additional half-day meetings were called. Company problems and opportunities were discussed over and over again, but few decisions were made. Departmental activities and overall performance suffered, and the company began to lose money for the first time in many years.

As for us, we found it difficult to develop our strategic plan because the executives with whom we needed to talk were busy attending the president's many conferences. We recommended to the president that he devote himself to long-range planning and public relations and appoint a chief operating officer who would have authority to manage company operations on a day-to-day basis consistent with approved budgets and company policy.

The president, instead of acting promptly on this suggestion or tabling it firmly, followed his usual pattern and talked it over with all the other company executives. Thereupon these executives began to contend among themselves for the COO position. Before the president could bring himself to decide among them or abandon the plan, the ablest of the executive group accepted a position as general manager of a competitor.

At this point, the board of directors stepped in and urged the president to appoint a general manager. With this impetus, the president selected the executive who seemed to be the least controversial. Even though we suspected that this executive was also the least competent, he was more decisive than the president, and the company's performance improved.

Unwillingness to Make Improvements Because They Will Be Costly

Sometimes an executive will recognize the need for an improvement but hesitate to make the expenditure involved in putting the improvement into practice, feeling that the company cannot be sure of an adequate return on the investment. In many cases, the indirect losses are considerably greater than the projected expenditure.

A few years ago we were engaged by a client in a service industry to study its customer service performance. The quality of services varied from location to location. When field personnel were questioned about poor service at their locations, their stock answer was, "Give us more people and we will do a better job." Since the company had never established cost standards for units of service, the headquarters executives had no effective rebuttal. Training programs had provided temporary improvements, but these improvements had been short-lived, because the company had no way of holding field management accountable for either quality or costs.

We recommended establishing a performance system that would measure both quality and costs in terms of volume of activity. The client agreed that these standards were needed, but feared that the expense of developing, installing, and maintaining such a system could not be justified. We pointed out the favorable results that other clients had achieved by the use of similar systems, but this client still did not act on our recommendation. The company's unit costs remain high, and the quality of its customer service continues to vary from location to location; its market share and earnings do not compare favorably with competitor's.

Interference from the CEO's Ego

It sometimes happens that, when a company's chief executive officer has experienced considerable success over a long period of time, he begins to think of himself as infallible. He takes major risks without much deliberation. If his ventures begin to go wrong, he is unwilling to admit his mistakes and take prompt corrective action. The

other company executives may see danger looming, but they fear that, if they protest, they will
rouse the CEO's ire and lose their positions. Even
consultants, although somewhat less vulnerable,
are seldom eager to tell a company chief that he
is on the wrong track.

Here is a case in point. A client, having been
extremely successful in areas where his company
was well-established, expanded their operations
to many other locations in the United States and
abroad within a short period of time. He did this
without conducting a serious evaluation of the
requirements for trained executives and other
personnel for the new locations and the need for
new capital for labor, real estate and merchan-
dise. The borrowing power of his company permitted the establishment of a huge debt that, even
on a long-term basis, required a considerable annual payment for interest and for debt retire-
ments. Profits plummeted. For the first time, the
company began to experience losses.

Many subordinate executives believed that the
company should move promptly to reduce the
number of new outlets, but the CEO refused to
even discuss the suggestion. Remembering that
he had been a client of ours, friends of mine in

the organization asked that I try to get through to him.

I set up a meeting on another pretext. Soon the conversation got around to the company's expansion. I spoke frankly.

"We all know that the company is losing money in many, if not most, of the new outlets," I said. "Why not close the losers, take your losses, and realize what you can before it is too late?"

The CEO was entirely unruffled. "Henry," he said, "you don't know what you're talking about. We have already taken the losses and are on the verge of the biggest boom the company has ever experienced."

I admitted that it was possible that I was wrong. "Nevertheless," I said, "it might be wise to have our firm, or another, evaluate performance in the new locations," so that he would have a second opinion. He rejected the idea completely. There was nothing more I could do.

The company's losses continued to increase. A year later, the board of directors asked for the CEO's resignation. He was replaced by an executive who at once began the process of disposing of unprofitable outlets to salvage what he could of a formerly highly successful company.

Expansion into Unfamiliar Fields

Managements that have been successful in running a company in an industry that they know well sometimes come to believe that they can manage any type of business in any industry. This is not likely to be true. Each industry is almost certain to have unique features that are critical for successful performance in that industry. Ignorance of these special factors often causes large conglomerates that have grown rapidly through mergers and acquisitions, to have difficulty in managing some of their new subsidiaries.

The problems of a client that acquired a food company as part of a group of companies illustrate this danger. This client had a long and successful history in the drug industry. The acquired food company had geographic coverage of the Midwest, but no brand franchise that would require the retail outlets to carry the products. In other words, its products were not so popular that customers would demand them. It had generated a reasonable level of profits by supplying good products, maintaining friendly relations with wholesalers and retailers, and carrying out frequent in-store promotions, including discounts, which assured its products of adequate shelf space.

Its management kept a tight control over costs. When our client company acquired it, the food company was earning several million dollars per year.

The new owner asked us to develop a strategic plan for its new subsidiary. After studying the situation, we recommended that the company continue using the marketing techniques that had been successful in the past, and in the meanwhile evaluate the expenditure for promotion, advertising and packaging that would be required to turn its products into market leaders. If the company decided on this course, we recommended that it proceed gradually, first instituting the new program in one region and later going on to others if the initial effort was a success.

In the meantime, our client company had brought in a new chief executive for the food company. This executive had an excellent record with another company. It was, indeed, a similar food company, but an extremely successful one that promoted its products heavily and was number one in the marketplace.

The new chief executive, confident that the methods that had worked at his former company would also be successful at this one, told our client that he had no need of our assistance or our plan.

He initiated a limited advertising campaign, but before it had a chance to take effect, he took action to eliminate the in-store promotions, and neglected the cultivation of the distributors and retailers. Some of the area stores stopped handling the company's products, and others reduced the shelf space allotted to them.

Sales declined precipitously, and severe losses resulted. To stop the bleeding, the parent company was forced to sell the subsidiary. It eventually found a buyer, but the selling price was considerably less than the value of the company at the time our client acquired it.

Inadequate Problem-Solving Actions

It is not uncommon for a client to agree in theory with a consultant's recommendations but to underestimate the amount of effort that will be required to put them into effect. When an undesirable condition has been in existence for some time, company executives usually work out a way to operate within its limits. To get them to change long-established habits and perform differently is likely to require more than just a verbal direction from headquarters.

Take the case of a service business that had a long history of conducting much of its labor relations activity on a highly centralized basis, with its corporate labor relations staff reporting to the chief executive.

The nature of its business required the company to have branches throughout the United States. All of its employees, except for management and sales personnel, were members of the same three unions. Labor negotiations took place at corporate headquarters. There was little input from field management. As new agreements were reached, they were mailed to the field with inadequate instructions or interpretation. All grievances were supposed to be settled at headquarters.

The field managers found this settlement procedure extremely cumbersome. Accordingly, they were in the habit of settling labor problems informally and locally, without necessarily following the terms of the contract. As a result, over the years labor practices had developed at the local level that were at variance with contract terms and with each other. Even the various supervisors at a single location would establish different practices.

Our firm was engaged to bring some order into the situation. After our study, we recommended that line management have the final authority in labor negotiations, with the Industrial Relations Department serving as staff. We also recommended that the company take steps to make its labor practices consistent in the field. The company was to give local management the authority to settle uncomplicated grievances, with guidance from the local Industrial Relations staff assigned to and directed by the chief local executive. We suggested that a training program for both line and staff management be developed to install the new approach, and offered to carry out the training ourselves.

The client accepted our organizational recommendations. However, its management believed that company personnel could develop and carry out the training program and that no further assistance was needed from us.

Two years later, although all the procedures we recommended had theoretically been adopted, company performance in labor relations had not changed substantially. The company trainers had not fully understood the subject matter and intent of the agreed-upon plan of action or the extent of the change in behavior patterns that would be involved in carrying it out.

Let me close this recital of disasters by reiterating that such management errors are not common. Most of the executives I have known have acted wisely much more often than not, to judge by the success of their companies. I do believe, however, that the above situations are typical of those in which even the most able of managements fail to understand or properly evaluate the results of their action or inaction.

CHAPTER

10

TRENDS
IN
CONSULTING

The past few years have seen rapid and sweeping changes both in the technological arena and in the economic and political climate, and there is no reason to believe that the rest of the twentieth century will be any less turbulent. Under these circumstances it is difficult to be sure which types of enterprise and which functional areas can be most benefited by consulting help in the immediate future, but there are a few obvious candidates. I would recommend that any executive directing any of the enterprises or functions described below review his or her needs to see whether outside assistance might be useful.

Enterprises That May Have Problems

Any sort of enterprise, of course, may run into difficulty at any time. There are certain classes of activity, however, that face particularly challenging situations at the present time.

Mature Companies. A company whose products have been successful in the marketplace for some time often finds it difficult to increase growth and profits. It may try to increase sales by bringing out extensions of or variations on its product line and by spending large sums on advertising and promotion, but its profit margins are likely to be small. This is particularly true where the competition is intense, as in the soft goods field. To improve its position it must better its marketing, manufacturing, distribution methods, or products. As time goes by, company staff exhausts its ideas.

A general management consulting firm equipped to make an overall survey can bring a fresh eye to the company's activities and may discover previously overlooked improvement opportunities. Such a firm can usually supply consultants to give assistance that may be required in particular areas of specialization, or specialist firms may be called in when the areas requiring improvement have been identified.

Companies That Have Grown Large Through Merger or Acquisition. A company that has recently acquired a partner or one or more subsidiaries of almost its own size is bound to have some difficulty in forging all of its units into a coherent whole, with a sound organization that provides proper policies and distribution of authority and responsibility, and effective performance controls. One of its main problems will be feelings of alienation and insecurity on the part of its employees, particularly those of the acquired company or companies.

A general management consultant who can conduct an overall diagnostic study of the combined businesses to identify the kind of organization and policies required can be very helpful to such a company, as can a human resources consultant, who can help with taking the steps and establishing the policies needed to make all the employees identify with the new company.

Businesses Affected by Changes in Government Regulations. As everyone concerned with such businesses knows, the recent radical changes in government regulations affecting certain types of enterprises have made enormous differences in their operating methods and problems. Particularly affected are banks, other financial institutions, and companies in the transportation field, such as airlines, railroads, and truckers. The financial institutions are in many cases responding by branching out into new fields. The long-established transportation companies, finding themselves in much more competitive situations than previously, are seeking to improve their skills in marketing, cost reduction, employee communications, and financial planning and control. The newer companies require assistance in establishing a consistent level of service.

Both general management consultants and specialists can be useful to all these companies, the generalists in defining overall actions needed for successful competition, and the specialists in areas such as human resources or marketing.

Small and Growing Companies. Although the executives of small companies, high-tech or not, are thoroughly familiar with their own fields and usually have little difficulty in finding out what their competitors are doing, they may need help in identifying what actions are needed to ensure growth and greater profitability.

Executives in charge of such companies may not always realize how much a consultant can do for them. Although most of my own experience has been with larger organizations, our firm once undertook a marketing study, at something less than our usual rates, for the owner of a manufacturing company whose sole product was a small engineering device. We discovered that the company was pricing the item much lower than necessary and recommended raising the price. The owner adopted our recommendations, with the result that the company increased its profits substantially and was able to expand into other types of business that we had suggested, also with good results.

Growing companies may need a consultant specializing in finance to advise on how best to underwrite their growth. As they continue to grow they may profitably use consulting assistance in other areas—organization planning, marketing, compensation, etc.

Various Branches of Government. Consultants can be of use to governmental bodies in a number of ways, such as conducting surveys, for the development of information to support policies and programs, and for many other purposes, including providing additional manpower. Although there are frequent drives to cut back on governmental use of consultants, such drives are always short-lived. As the size of government grows, the use of consultants cannot avoid growing with it. The need for their help will continue in the foreseeable future.

Executives employed by branches of the federal government usually find it more convenient to employ consultants based in the Washington area. These consultants are familiar with the governmental environment. They know what may and may not be done, and who may do it. They are personally acquainted with many of the executives in the various government departments as well as with congressmen and senators and with employees of congressional committees. They are accustomed to the competitive bidding system by which many government departments must award consulting contracts. Many consultants based in other cities are not familiar with this process and find it a difficult and expensive way to do business. Consultants of all types, whether specialist or generalist, can be found in the Washington area.

State and local governments need consultants for the same reasons that the federal government does. Some county governments, with which I am familiar, have been accustomed to use consultants to conduct surveys of all kinds, carry out environmental studies, develop information

needed to establish policies or programs, and so
forth. For local political reasons, it is frequently
convenient to use consultants to make determi-
nations on controversial matters.

Functional Areas in Which
Consultants Will Be Most Needed

As I have already suggested, I believe that now
and in the near future many companies are or
will be in need of the kinds of services tradition-
ally performed by general management consultants: organization planning, overall surveys, and
so on. In addition, there are three areas of consultant specialization that seem particularly important in today's conditions.

Human Resources. As business and government
have grown, employing more and more people
in the process, employee identification with the
employing entity has weakened. It has also become more difficult for the employer to evaluate
performance fairly, to identify comers in the organization, to develop people and motivate them
to work for common goals, to compensate employees equitably, and to set up fair and appropriate personnel policies and ensure that they are

uniformly interpreted. Also, in fields such as the airline and automobile industries, where unions have long been strong and where competition has recently become a more significant factor, management often needs skilled help to secure employee understanding of the new conditions.

As mentioned previously, there has been considerable interest lately in the Japanese Quality Circle concept, which brings lower-level employees and management together in a way different from that traditional in the United States. The German concept of board of directors memberships for unions has also been adopted in some instances.

Human resources specialists who are familiar with the ins and outs of the new approaches, and also those skilled in the more traditional techniques of establishing equitable compensation and benefit policies, personnel administration practices, and so on, can make important contributions to the welfare of corporate and governmental giants.

Communications. Internal communications have been revolutionized by the introduction of computer-based information systems and various other technological wonders. Systems based on the new technology offer a wide variety of opportunities to improve company performance, lower costs, and encourage growth. Along with providing more complete and up-to-date information, they make it possible to eliminate extra levels of organization, conduct interbranch conferences via video, and maintain two-way communication with workers at all levels.

Consultants who are skilled in the new techniques can contribute importantly to company health and welfare.

Manufacturing. As I pointed out in an earlier chapter, in recent years there has been a tendency at top management levels to take manufacturing operations for granted and to concentrate executive attention on more glamorous areas, such as marketing. Today, many companies need help not only in improving manufacturing efficiency through such techniques as robotics but also in restoring the manufacturing function to its proper place in the company hierarchy.

General management consultants are today turning their attention to this field, and are particularly helpful in integrating it properly with the other management processes. There are also a number of excellent consulting firms that specialize in manufacturing and distribution and are knowledgeable about the new methodologies.

I do not, of course, mean to imply by any of the previous suggestions that other traditional specialties, such as marketing, corporate planning, systems development, and others, are in danger of losing their usefulness. It is simply that I believe that there is a greater need for improvement in the areas just discussed.

Know When to Stop

To conclude this discussion of the consulting process, I would like to offer one final word of advice: Do not overuse consultants or keep them at work any longer than necessary. Before you call the consultant in, make sure that there is a real need for his or her services; do everything possible to see that the consultant produces viable recommendations promptly; and then act on those recommendations without undue delay.

If those suggestions are followed, I am sure that you will find working with consultants an enlightening, profitable and generally rewarding experience.

INDEX

THE AUTHOR

Henry Golightly is a well-known management consultant. He and his firm, Golightly & Co. International, Inc., specialized in general management consulting, organizational development, human resources planning (including the establishment of Quality Circles), strategic planning, executive search, and related matters. Particularly, the firm was active in the airline industry and service-oriented and marketing companies. Mr. Golightly was chairman and chief executive officer of Golightly & Co. from 1959 until its merger with Harbridge House in 1979. Earlier in his career he was a principal of McKinsey & Co. for ten years.

Mr. Golightly was born in Texas, attended the University of Texas, and is a graduate of the South Texas School of Law, with a Doctorate of Jurisprudence. He is a member of the Texas Bar Association as well as the American Bar Association. He is a Certified Management Consultant and a past director of the Association of Consulting Management Engineers.

Mr. Golightly is the author of the book *Managing with Style*. He has lectured and published numerous articles on many phases of business management. He has served on a number of boards of directors and is currently on the board of Kay Laboratories in London and Young & Rubicam Coudrey in Australia, as well as Just One Break and the Youth Counseling League in New York. Mr. Golightly has conducted seminars on management consulting for MBA candidates at Columbia University.